ALL OUR KIN

Carol Stack

BasicBooks
A Subsidiary of Perseus Books, L.L.C.

*Dedicated with respect and admiration to my
parents, Ruth and Isadore Berman, to my friend
"Ruby Banks," and to the other people of The
Flats*

The table on pp. 102, 103, appears in the author's essay, "The Kindred
of Viola Jackson: Residence and Family Organization of an Urban Black
American Family," pp. 303–312, in *Afro-American Anthropology: Contemporary Perspectives*, edited by N. E. Whitten and John F. Szwed,
copyright © 1970, used with the permission of The Free Press, a division
of Macmillan and Company.

Designed by Janice Stern

First HARPER PAPERBACK published 1975. Reissued by BasicBooks, 1997.

ISBN: 0–06–131982–1

01 00   RRD-H 50 49 48 47 46 45 44

CONTENTS

Charts and Tables

CHARTS

TABLES

Acknowledgments

I wish to acknowledge the important influence and example of several people. My most devoted discussant and tireless co-researcher in the field study is John R. Lombardi, whose participation in the analysis of field data was invaluable and whose keen understanding of social forces make this work as much his as mine. I am pleased that he agreed to co-author the conclusions to this book.

I wish to thank F. K. Lehman for his time and knowledge in discussing the issues raised here, and Edward Bruner for his intellectual and emotional support during my graduate studies. I am also indebted to Nancie Gonzalez, Eva Hunt, Dimitri Shimkin, John Stack, Charles Valentine and Betty Lou Valentine, Norman Whitten, and the late Oscar Lewis for encouragement, counsel, and criticism.

I am grateful to Douglas Butterworth, Joseph Casagrande, Louise Lamphere, Marcella Mazzarelli, Jenny Phillips, David Plath, Bill Ringle, Herbert Semmel, and Robert Weiss for helpful comments on preliminary versions of the manuscript, and to Troy Armstrong, Marty Beaumont, Myra Bluebond, Susan Cobb, Peter Hainer, Norma Linton, Douglas Midgett, Duane Orlowski, Mimi Rodin, and Brett Williams, all of whom have been helpful and generous with their time. Sonya Salamon provided excellent research assistance in the early stages, and sympathy and support during the entire course of the study. Shirley Wattenberg offered continual support and assistance in the initial stages of the case history survey of welfare families. I owe a special debt of thanks to Marion Brinkerhoff who typed endless versions of this manuscript over the past three years.

I would also like to thank my colleagues at the Child Development Laboratory, Queenie Mills and Molly Mowrer, for their friendship and encouragement. Warm thanks to Jeannette Hopkins of Harper & Row for her editorial and intellectual guidance in the preparation of the manuscript.

My three-year-old son Kevin was a wholehearted participant in the research effort, and comforting to me in moments of stress.

I am deeply grateful to the people of The Flats who gave their cooperation and friendship.

This research was supported by the Department of Health, Education, and Welfare (MH 12247-01).

Introduction

This introduction anticipates curiosity about how a young white woman could conduct a study of black family life, and provides a basis for evaluating the reliability and quality of the data obtained.

The questions raised relate to a broad spectrum of questions fundamental to social analysis. Is it possible for an outsider who symbolizes the dominant culture to enter a black community, win the community's participation and approval, acquire reliable data, and judge its reliability? What roles can the researcher assume? Can the observer grasp how his questions are interpreted by the informants? Can the observer discover rules used by those studied for managing their daily affairs? Can the observer distinguish his own theories for making sense of the data from the meanings given by community members in their everyday life? How do the initial channels chosen to gain an entrée into a community affect the findings and biases of an anthropological field study?

In both industrial and nonindustrial societies, researchers have typically established their first contacts with men who hold power—the colonial administrators, tribal chiefs, local mayors, and judges. These men draw upon their status in the community and favors owed to them to usher the researchers into the community, the first link in what becomes a chain of introductions. Anyone proceeding through other channels runs the risk of offending those in power and provoking an invitation to leave the community.

Within most black communities in the United States today, power is divided among the older generation of professionals in the black establishment and the younger activist leaders and organizations. I could have gained my first contacts in The Flats by working through the established network of black men and women who had status and power in The Flats and in the larger community of Jackson Harbor. In the mid-sixties two other white social scientists had entered the black community in Jackson Harbor through contacts with preachers, teachers, social workers, and other black professionals. Although they were not conducting a study requiring intensive participant–observer techniques, their research was confined and limited. They came into contact only with individuals and families chosen by the black establishment to represent the community: churchgoers, families on good terms with their social workers, and those men and women who had obtained legal marriages. Even more decisive as a handicap was their identification, in the eyes of those studied, with those black leaders who personally derived their status and importance from their acceptance within the white community. They were regarded as "uppity" individuals who "thought they were too good to sit down on an old couch."

When I first began this study in the mid-sixties, the community itself had produced a few articulate, intellectual spokesmen against racial and political injustice. Their speeches and their activities were aimed primarily at the white community. Within the black community itself, they were not controlling voices. I later came to know the young men and women involved in political activism within the black community as I became committed to their causes: a free health center, a Welfare Rights Organization, a job-training center, black businesses. Many of these individuals whom I met in the initial stages of this research later became members of activist organizations in The Flats. Such persons may, in the future, decide whether a research study of their community may be conducted and by whom. They may choose to censor findings that they believe may be used to repress, harm, or manipulate those studied.

Some of my colleagues strongly advised me to enter the black community through the older black establishment; they cited various reasons: contacts were available; the research setting, they argued, was physically dangerous to a white person and I might need the sponsorship and protection that such contacts could provide; and tradition dictated such a procedure. I decided instead to find my own means of entrée. I decided to circumvent the obvious centers of influence—the pastors, the politicians—and try to reach families without resorting to middlemen. Through my own efforts and good luck I came to know a young woman who had grown up on welfare in The Flats and had since come to my university. She agreed to introduce me to families she had known as she was growing up there. She would introduce me to two unrelated families and from then on I would be on my own.

In time I knew enough people well who were closely related so that after any family scene, gathering, or fight, I could put together interpretations of the events from the viewpoints of different individuals, particularly in instances when there were conflicts over rights in children. In addition to taking multiple observations of each event myself, I eventually asked others to assist me in the study. I found three Flats residents (two women and a man) who participated as part-time and casual assistants in the project. I selected individuals from the families I knew, who were interested in the study, and who were imaginative and critical thinkers. At times these assistants became "informants," in the language of anthropology, that is, they provided me with data. Together we worked out questions on various topics to ask the families studied. The research schedules used in this book (see Appendix B) are an outcome of mutual attempts by my assistants and myself to map out meaningful questions about daily life in the community.

We selected questions in the general areas of social and domestic relations, kinship and residence, and child-keeping;

these questions provided a starting point for long discussions on a single issue. At no time did I formally interview anyone. I taped informal conversations after an event, when I was alone with someone I knew very well and with permission, asking that the situation be related to me from that person's point of view. This offered a check against my own field notes. The quoted passages chosen for this book represent, to my thinking, my common-sense model of the individuals I studied in The Flats. The theoretical perspectives that helped me to order the data I gathered can be divided into three central concerns: how people are recruited to kin networks; the relationship between household composition and residence patterns; and the relationship between reciprocity and poverty. The rationale for selecting these perspectives emerges in the course of the book.

Because of the personal nature of the information obtained about individuals, and the promise that this information would be confidential, it was necessary to disguise the names of the informants. I gave a fictitious name to each person whose name or life entered into the study. Even when I tried out my own assumptions and interpretations of events on my friends and assistants, I used fictitious names for the examples.

The people that I studied in The Flats use first names in one another's presence, and to refer to their neighbors and friends. Surnames are used infrequently and often people do not know the surnames of long-time acquaintances and friends, although the coining of nicknames for siblings and friends is a creative and endless pastime. Nicknames personalize and endear; they dramatically expose memorable or striking characteristics about a person, giving him a very special identity. I also acquired several nicknames during the study, but the one that held was "white Caroline," a name originally given to me by a family to distinguish me from their niece whose name was also Caroline. (My real name, Carol, was always pronounced

Caroline). She became known as "black Caroline" soon after the children in her family began calling me "white Caroline." I first discovered this nickname one afternoon when I phoned the family and a youngster who answered the phone called out, "Mama, white Caroline's on the phone."

To retain the flavor of daily communication, I have chosen to use first names in this book after people are initially introduced. Surnames are used in The Flats primarily when residents deal with the whites who enter the community as social workers, landlords, or teachers who assume asymmetrical relationships to Flats' residents.

In the life histories presented in this book, a person's job, family size, and the intimate events in life histories have been changed so that no one would be recognizable. Likewise, The Flats is a fictitious name, as is the name of the city, Jackson Harbor. The statistics cited on the community are derived from the U.S. Census (1960–1970), but in order to conceal the identity of the city, the figures have been slightly obscured. Nonetheless, the description depicts the setting, and accurately characterizes numerous other urban areas in the Midwest and the ghetto quarters within these towns.

Although the community assistants never asked many of the questions they generated (see Appendix B), their questions provided me with a perspective on their explanation and perception of a variety of behavior patterns in The Flats. This procedure provided one form of data, one of the many methodological devices tried in the study. Cicourel (1964, p. 61) develops this method in his book *Method and Measurement in Sociology*. He says, "The scientific observer must take into account the common-sense constructs employed by the actor in everyday life if he is to grasp the meanings that will be assigned by the actor to his questions, regardless of the form in which they are presented to the actor."

It is very often difficult for social scientists to comprehend the impact of institutional racism on black life. This is suggested by Joyce Ladner (1971; 6) in the Introduction to her study of black adolescent girls, *Tomorrow's Tomorrow*. "It has been argued," Ladner writes, "that the relationship between the *researcher* and his *subjects*, by definition, resembles that of the oppressor and the oppressed, because it is the oppressor who defines the problem, the nature of the research and, to some extent, the quality of the interaction between him and his subjects. This inability to understand and research the fundamental problem—*neo-colonialism*—prevents most social researchers from being able accurately to observe and analyze black life and culture and the impact racism and oppression has upon Blacks." Recently there have been attempts by social scientists to overcome some of these difficulties, and to understand the true nature of the relationship between the economic system and the lives of black people.

Members of a culture have biases that affect their perceptions of themselves and their life ways; outsiders bring biases to the cultures they study. Although life experiences produce a difference in perceptions, these perceptions can be shared. The three years I spent in The Flats opened and reassembled my life ways and my understanding of womanhood, parenthood, and the American economy. Likewise, I brought perceptions and biases to the study that joggled and molded the views of those closest to me.

A researcher in the social sciences is practically always defined as an outsider in a study, even if he or she has close attachment and commitment to the community, and shares a similar cultural background. Even a study of the culture of one's most intimate associations—our friends, colleagues, or kin—thrusts the researcher apart. Whether studying elites, bureaucracy, or the poor, if one hopes to discover the rules of routine behavior, the observer himself must attempt to learn how to move appropriately inside the private world of those observed. The researcher must take time and patience and practice, attempting to reduce the distance between the model outsiders used to explain social order and the explanations employed by those studied. Attempts will fail, but this prodding hopefully will bring the observer to an intimate point of contact in the study whereby he becomes both an actor and a subject whose learned definitions can themselves be analyzed.[1]*

* Notes to the chapters begin on p. 155.

"*Although there was always generosity in the Negro neighborhood, it was indulged on pain of sacrifice. Whatever was given by Black people to other Blacks was most probably needed as desperately by the donor as by the receiver. A fact which made the giving or receiving a rich exchange.*"
—I Know Why the Caged Bird Sings,
Maya Angelou

THE FLATS

THE SETTING

The Flats is the poorest section of a black community in the Midwestern city of Jackson Harbor (these names are fictitious). The city of Jackson Harbor is on a major rail line connecting Chicago and several Southern states, the way north for many of the black people who came to The Flats from the South in the thirties and forties. The railroad remained a relatively cheap and convenient means of keeping contacts alive with relatives in the South and with friends and relatives in Chicago. Kin and friends in Chicago are important to people in The Flats, for they provide a model for an urbanized life style, contacts for exchange of goods, and reduce the sense of isolation often felt by a repressed minority in a small city.

The past fifty years have witnessed a similar migration of rural, Southern Blacks to other urban centers in the United States. Between 1940 and 1960 many thousands of farms in the South disappeared, and three and a half million black people left the South for a new life in the cities. Many of the first hopeful participants in this great migration are now middle-aged or elderly residents who have lived a lifetime in poverty and now see their grandchildren entrapped in the same poverty-stricken conditions.

According to the U.S. Census Jackson Harbor is ranked as an "urbanized area" since its population exceeds 50,000. A rather large state-run hospital is the city's major employer. Yet, only 3 percent of its 5,000 employees are black, compared to the city's population of more than 12 percent black. And, by and large, even those 3 percent hold the most menial jobs. In recent years intensive efforts by liberal groups to increase the percentage of black employees have been totally unsuccessful. There is little industry in Jackson Harbor. An industrial company, employing almost 2,500 people, more than half women, recently closed down. A food processing factory with about 800 employees provides most of the industrial employment for black men. The strongly segregated craft and construction unions permit few Blacks to hold jobs in their industries.

In 1968, a year of record economy in the country, unemployment among Blacks in Jackson Harbor was more than 20 percent. Among those working, more than 63 percent were service workers—maids, cooks, janitors, and the like. In 1959, while 80 percent of the "white" families made more than $4,000 a year, 60 percent of the "non-white" families (data is so labeled) made less. Those who found work were often not significantly better off than those without work who were eligible for welfare benefits.

Jackson Harbor has been rated one of the ten most expensive cities in the United States. The income necessary for a family of four has been estimated at more than $8,000. In terms of average family income, the county which includes Jackson Harbor ranks in the highest twenty nationwide. Most of the white population who have chosen to live in Jackson Harbor can afford to live there. Few of the Blacks can.

Most families live in one- and two-family houses and scattered multiple dwellings. Apartments are few, and there are no large public housing projects. Although larger old homes in The Flats have been subdivided into tiny, inadequate apartments, the population density is much lower there than in a typical urban environment such as Chicago. But for the Blacks in The Flats, as in many such ghetto communities, crowding is severe nonetheless. Most homes in The Flats are small, wood-framed houses, bungalows, and shacks in need of major repairs. There are too many people for the available room. The streets are spotted with small grocery stores, poorly stocked and expensive, and house-front churches, barbers, bars, snack shops, sweet shops, and hat shops. The streets and front yards are cluttered with broken glass, beer cans, and old cars. Old tires and bed springs fill back yards. Porch doors, screens, and broken windows go unfixed. During the winter snowstorms, the streets in The Flats, many of them unpaved, gravel streets, are the last in the city to be cleared. Although temperatures go below zero in Jackson Harbor without fail every winter, many houses have doors and windows that do not fit tightly. A common trick to seal cracks in the window casements is to fill them with water on a freezing day to provide a frigid seal until the first thaw.

While only 10 percent of the Whites in the town live in housing termed "deteriorating" and 1 percent live in housing termed "dilapidated," by the Census of 1960, among Blacks, 26 percent live in deteriorating housing and 13 percent in dilapidated, unfit housing. I visited only few houses that were not roach-infested. In one home roaches exceeded one per square foot on all of the walls inside the house. Children sleeping in this house were covered with sores and scabs from insect bites.

Health care for Blacks in Jackson Harbor is also predictably inadequate. Until recently the few white doctors who would take black patients held separate office hours for them in the evenings in order not to offend their white patients. A free health clinic, supported by state health funds, recently opened in The Flats, but communication within The Flats concerning the clinic is poor and few people use it. Despite increasing public assistance for medical needs, many black people put off seeing a doctor as long as possible. Feelings of mistrust run deep.

The ways in which the poor die reflect the conditions of their lives. In 1965 more than 9.1 percent of the deaths among non-whites were caused by diseases of early infancy; only 4.6 percent of the deaths among Whites were infant diseases. More than 10 percent of non-white deaths were due to accidents or homicide, as compared with less than 5 percent for Whites.

Dental care is equivalent in mediocrity to medical care. Few Blacks over the age of twenty-five have many of their original teeth. It is not uncommon to find people who had all their teeth pulled on their first visit to the dentist.

Among young women this usually occurred when they were in their early twenties and covered by the same AFDC health benefits as their young children.

Many more statistics could be added, but they would simply repeat the same depressing patterns of the black situation in any "urbanized area" in the country. In all their contacts with the dominant white culture, Blacks in Jackson Harbor are treated with some form of institutional or personalized racism. At best this takes the form of overt, benign paternalism. At worst the reminders are in the form of bullets. In the last three years, in widely publicized cases, two Blacks in the community were murdered by white policemen. Both victims were about to be arrested for charges no more severe than speeding, and neither was armed. Each policeman faced a hearing but no punishment was decreed. No Black in The Flats was surprised.

Yet despite the similarities between economic, political, and racist forces in Jackson Harbor and those of the inner-city slums, people in The Flats think their lives are better than the lives of their friends and relatives in Chicago. An elderly woman residing in The Flats recalls that many years ago before she and her husband left Arkansas, people said to her, "If you want to lose your man just go North." Today she qualifies this advice. "If you stay out of Chicago there is a chance a woman can hold her man." Although there are few alternatives, and no funds to move elsewhere, many people living in The Flats say that they have chosen to live there.

THE RESEARCH SCENE

I was introduced to two families, one from Arkansas, one from Mississippi. First there was the household of Viola and Leo Jackson. Between 1916 and 1967 ninety-six of Viola and Leo's kin left Arkansas plantations to live and work in the fruit-harvesting areas around Grand Rapids and Benton Harbor, Michigan, and Racine, Wisconsin; eventually most of their kin settled in the urban North, especially in The Flats in Jackson Harbor.

Viola and Leo Jackson have lived in The Flats with their eleven children since their arrival from Arkansas fifteen years ago. They are buying a small, wood-framed, five-room house, an old house in need of repair and improvement. The linoleum on the living room and kitchen floors is cracked and pitted and the ill-fitted wooden beams admit freezing drafts in the severe cold of the Midwestern winters and insects throughout the humid summers. The inside walls are streaked with unfinished paint jobs, and the house is bare of decoration except for one knickknack shelf that holds empty medicine bottles, a trophy, and a picture of Viola's dead brother.

Before coming to The Flats Leo worked picking cotton and harvesting fruit. Today he is a hod carrier in a local laborers' union and receives a minimum wage guarantee when he is working, but the work is seasonal and Leo spends most of his days waiting at the union hiring hall to be called on a job. Viola works occasionally as a cook on the swing swift in a local restaurant in Jackson Harbor which pays $1.10 an hour. She works for a month or so and then quits without notice either because she cannot stand on her feet any longer, or because a child is sick at home. The Jacksons' oldest son drives a taxi part-time, their oldest daughter accepts seasonal work at a local factory, and a son in high school washes dishes after school. (When the oldest son was drafted, the mother wanted me to seek exemption on the ground that his job was necessary.) The adults arrive home at odd hours of the day, making it impossible for them to have meals together—indeed, it is rare for a house to have enough chairs for everyone to sit down at one time—but they still see one another every day, if only in the late hours talking and drowsing with television, radio, and records in the background, often playing simultaneously. The young boys and girls spend a great deal of time practicing any of a dozen or so new dance steps—like the Funky Chicken, the Strutting Rooster, and the Gold Digger—circulating in The Flats from Chicago. Because a neighbor is a Pentecostal minister, the Jacksons draw their shades in order not to offend him.

The family's total income varies from year to year, but the family has earned in recent years no more than $4,500 in any one year (including minimal Aid to Families with Dependent Children Support). Gross family expenditures for the Jacksons, including mortgage payments, insurance, cars, food, and utilities amount to approximately $3,500. This leaves between $500 and $1,000, depending on earnings, for clothes, house repairs, medical expenses, and miscellaneous expenditures for a household of fourteen people (since the addition of a grandson).

The rooms are crowded but clean. Each child in the family has his own chores to do—the teen-age boys wash floors, the girls cook and clean the kitchen, and the younger children— ten- and eleven-year-olds—take the family laundry to the laundromat. By 9:00 A.M. every bed in the house is made. Except in a household with only young children, the adult role is primarily one of training and supervision. There are bunk beds and an old metal frame bed in the boys' room in the Jackson household, a couch and a double bed in the girls' room (two or three children sleep together), and a double bed in the parents' room. Privacy is impossible.

Social space assumes great importance in a crowded living area. This is true of the Jackson family and other families as well. The paucity of personal space leads to efforts by the adults, often extreme, to protect themselves from encroachments, and their space from violation, particularly by children. (This space varies according to a person's mood, but children are often kept as far as four or five feet away from adults.) A child who entered an adult's social space would be punished. The lack of privacy is distressing especially to teen-age girls. They spend more time at home, not on the streets in gangs as do their brothers, and until they establish their status as adults by having a child, they must share a bed and room with their younger sisters. When they have a child, they are accorded new privileges, for example, a bed to be shared only with their infant (in fact, even when the father is in the home, the infant shares their bed). Also, private space sometimes may be defined by a shower curtain or a bedspread hung as a partition.

Viola and Leo frequently see their relatives who are residing in The Flats, in neighboring counties, and in Chicago and St. Louis. A steady stream of relatives gathers daily in the Jackson home—Viola's seventy-year-old mother, Viola's children, their cousins and friends. In the mornings the mother visits, bringing along the three grandchildren she is raising. In the afternoons and on weekends Viola's brother and his two sons, and Leo's sister and brother and their families, visit. When relatives come unexpectedly from Chicago or St. Louis, it is the occasion for a big and festive meal. The women devote all day to preparing it. Fresh coconut is munched as an hors d'oeuvre before dinner. Dinner may be greens flavored with pig's knuckles, egg pie (like a quiche), sweet potatoes, and home-baked buttermilk biscuits. There may be raccoon shot by men of the neighborhood and sold door to door, but the Jacksons prefer chicken or turkey.

On an ordinary day, in the morning after the children leave for school and the adults for work, Viola is often lonely. The house is empty and quiet. During such hours, with little money to spend, no car, and little to do since the children have done the chores, Viola welcomes an attentive listener, a willing companion to take along visiting, shopping, or to the laundry. I tried to become such a listener and companion.

During my first visit Viola told me that she and her husband Leo have kept their family together for twenty-three years. Leo, she said, is a "good man, a man who works and brings his money home." After several week-day visits, Viola asked me to come over on a Sunday afternoon when the family would be home. The younger children and Viola had spoken of my visits and I was not surprised to encounter some hostility from Viola's older children and Leo's brother when I arrived. Viola called me back to the kitchen where the women were cooking a Sunday dinner. Verna, Viola's nineteen-year-old daughter, and I, both six months' pregnant, talked about names and nicknames for our babies, and eventually almost everyone in the household joined the conversation, even the young children, suggesting amusing combinations of names not only for family members. "Suppose your name was Bottom, how about Rosy Bottom? Or if it was Snap, how about Ginger Snap?" Last names are regarded as relatively unimportant; contacts among people are intimate visits rather than letter writing and there are few occasions to focus on formal identities. The tradition is oral. Names are not looked up in a phone book; numbers are memorized as are addresses and information about family financial matters.

The conversation among Verna, Viola, and myself was long, warm, and lively, and eased the strain. Our visits continued for many months.

One incident eased my communication with Viola's husband and his brother. Late one evening I was at the Jacksons' home, still pregnant, my cumbersome silhouette similar to Verna's. I was wearing dark tights and the rooms were poorly lighted, with the television providing the brightest rays. Leo, slumped down in his chair, called out to me, "Hey, Verna, get your baby his bottle so he'll stop his crying." Leo had confused me with Verna. He laughed so hard it was difficult to stop. From then on, when any relative or friend dropped by, Leo recounted this story. All their kin in The Flats—more than seventy people —heard it sooner or later.

My first year in The Flats was a period of intense observation and questioning of the familiar standard interpretations of black family life. I focused initially on the Jacksons' migration and the urban adjustment of ninety-six of their kin who had left rural Arkansas during the past fifty years and are now living in Chicago, St. Louis, or in The Flats. I began to notice a pattern of cooperation and mutual aid among kin during the migration North and formed a hypothesis that domestic functions are carried out for urban Blacks by clusters of kin who do not necessarily live together, and that the basis of these units is the domestic cooperation of close adult females and the exchange of goods and services between male and female kin (Stack 1970). This was the starting point for my study of the strategies for coping with poverty.

A year after I met the Jacksons and their kin, I met the family and friends of Magnolia and Calvin Waters and their network of kinsmen, which proved to number more than one hundred. Magnolia and her kin came from a background of urban poverty in the South. Before migrating to the North they had for the most part lived in a cluster of towns near Jackson, Mississippi. Calvin's family had been sharecroppers in rural Mississippi, but one by one he and his brothers moved northward, hoping to find secure jobs.

Magnolia Waters is a large, powerful, and resourceful woman with a regal composure. At forty-one, the mother of eleven, Magnolia appeared no older than her striking, articulate, twenty-three-year-old daughter, Ruby Banks. Magnolia's four sisters and two brothers and their families all live in The Flats and each of her sister's children has received public aid. The second generation of children born in The Flats, Magnolia's grandchildren, grandnieces and nephews, are also AFDC (Aid to Families with Dependent Children) recipients. (This is not surprising since a third of 188 AFDC mothers included in a survey of AFDC case histories for this study [see Appendix A] were themselves AFDC children.)

I first came by the Waters' home in the summer of 1968. Magnolia, her sixty-year-old "husband" Calvin (father of six of Magnolia's children), Magnolia's oldest son Lenny, and five of the younger children were sitting in the living room on a red velvet couch, which Magnolia had covered herself. The eight were methodically folding several piles of newspapers for Lenny's five evening paper routes, a daily family routine. (The pungent smell of newspaper print filled the room.) After a lesson from a seven-year-old on how to make the fold, I joined in on the rhythmic activity that ʾbsorbed everyone's concentration. It was an hour and a half before all of the newspapers were ready for delivery. Magnolia joked about my hands, black with newsprint. I told them I would like to begin a study of family life in The Flats. Magnolia and Calvin told me to come by again and to bring my baby.

Several months later Magnolia told me that she had been surprised that I sat with them that first day to fold papers, and then came back to help again. "White folks," she told me, "don't have time, they's always in a rush, and they don't sit on black folk's furniture, at least no Whites that comes into The Flats."

MY HOME BASE

The Jacksons' home with its seven children (living at home) became a home base, a place where I was welcome to spend the day, week after week, and where my year-old son Kevin and I could sleep, usually sharing a bed with children in the household. My personal network expanded naturally as I met those whom the Waters met or visited each day. My home base changed as I became personally accepted by others, and ultimately I was welcome at several unrelated households. These individuals and their personal networks radiated out to include more than three hundred people, whom I eventually visited, but I observed most intensively fifteen unrelated coalitions of kinsmen. In their homes my presence was least intrusive.

Through Magnolia and Calvin I met Magnolia's oldest daughter, Ruby Banks. Ruby was born in The Flats and raised "on aid" by her grandmother and Magnolia's sister, Augusta. Ruby is now raising her own children, also "on aid." Magnolia described Ruby's vitality and strong-headedness to me, warning that Ruby might be hostile to me, my whiteness, and my presence there. Nevertheless, I was anxious to meet Ruby, and Magnolia had become eager for us to meet.

The scene of our first meeting bristled with the tenseness of our anticipation. That very morning Magnolia and I had been casually chatting about the days before she met Calvin, and her relationship with James Henderson, the father of her oldest children. Ruby walked into Magnolia's house "cussing," "putting down" the mess and the dirt on the floor, and the clothes Magnolia's younger children had on that day. Then she saw me on the couch and my year-old son on the floor. "The dirt on the floor could kill a white baby," she said. Paying no attention, Magnolia continued our conversation, telling me how much Ruby looked like her father. Ruby pulled up a stool, sat down, and lectured to me in a high-pitched voice, "James Henderson, he's no father to me! I don't even speak to him. I don't really own him because of the way he did me. The only father I know is my stepfather Calvin, and there's no better man in the world."

Ruby was angry at Magnolia. Her description of the world in which Ruby lived was not Ruby's. She shook her head and shouted, "Don't you believe a word of what she says. If that's what Magnolia been telling you, you better come over to my house and get things straight the way I see them." At that point Magnolia chuckled to herself, grabbed my son's bottle, and yelled at one of the children to fill it. Ruby looked at my son, grunted, and said, "That boy should have been off the bottle six months ago."

When I visited Magnolia the following afternoon, she asked me to take Ruby's youngest daughter, who spent the night at her house, back over to Ruby's. Remembering Ruby's "invitation," I was happy to run the errand. Ruby shared a house with Magnolia's sister, Augusta, across town. This was the first of hundreds of trips I made across town as I began to participate in daily visiting patterns in The Flats.

When I arrived Ruby was wringing out hand-washed clothing in an old handwringer. Her five-year-old daughter was changing a baby's diaper, and her two younger children were playing on the porch. Ruby called me into the kitchen and together we finished wringing out at least ten pounds of wet clothing. When we sat down to rest, Ruby talked about her father.

"I first met my father when I was in the third or fourth grade. I was in a grocery store and my mother introduced me to him and he looked at me and said, 'You sure have grown,' and patted me on the head. I looked up at him and asked, 'Is that really my father?' Magnolia said yes. Easter was coming so I said to him, 'How about buying me a pair of shoes since you never have given me nothing in your life and you never did nothing for me?' He told me to come over to his house on Bell Street and ask for him and he would give me the money for the shoes. When I went it so happened he wasn't there. His wife came out and pushed me off the porch. I was small and she shook me and called me all kinds of low-down names and told me that I didn't have no father. Then she hauled off and hit me and pushed me in the car and told me never to come back there again.

"My mother knew my father's people and my Aunt Augusta is real good friends with Aunt Ann, my father's sister. Some of my father's people really took to me. Uncle Leon came around the house to see me when I was really small and that's how I got to know him. Aunt Ann welcomed me to her house anytime I got ready to go over there. She's the only one I go and see now, she and Aunt Betty. The rest of them are snobs and they don't care nothing about me. I have a half brother by my father and he cares lots for me. Whenever he sees me, if he got money he give it to me. My other half brother, he's just like his mother. He thinks he so much.

"I don't speak to my father, but when he sees me he still tells his friends that he own me—but he tells his wife that he don't have a daughter. I know I'm a Henderson, and there's no way that the law and nobody else can say differently, but my mother put her name on my birth certificate because she knew that I would hate my father when I grew up. Right today I wish that she had never told me who my father was.

"A child wants a father to play with, to laugh with, and to hug. I wouldn't give my stepfather up for anybody in this world. I really appreciate what he did for me. It reminds me of a record that came out called 'Color Him Father.' It's about a man who ran away from his wife and left her with their children. Then another man came into the picture and helped them out so much that they called him 'color him father.' That record speaks of my life. It reminds me of my real father and how he treated me and my mother. My mother couldn't hardly get him to buy a light bulb. But, he tells a different story about how much he loved my mother, so who's to say."

We began to talk about the difference between Magnolia's, Ruby's, and Ruby's father's explanations of their relationships. Ruby told me that to learn anything about her family, or family life in The Flats—in order to interpret any single event—I would have to talk to many people. I took her advice and it turned out to be wise.

During the following months Ruby and I began to spend a great deal of time together and with our children. Ruby's attitudes toward men, kin, friends, and children shook many of my views, and I am still in the process of reshaping them today. For her part Ruby would get mad, amazed, and amused at some of the views I held. Whenever I expressed hesitation or uneasiness about my own ability to make it alone, with my child, Ruby would get very angry, providing me with numerous examples of women around The Flats who were doing so. Ruby was probing, observing, and interpreting my perceptions just as I was doing with hers. At times over the three years of our friendship, we would find many ways to test our perceptions of one another.

Ruby and I enjoyed comparing our attitudes and approaches toward everything. Although she asked me to bring my white friends over to her house, she was always hypercritical in assessing whether they were anti-Black or whether they "put on airs." Some of my friends she liked very much, yet she encouraged me to break up some friendships, especially if she had reason to doubt a friend's loyalty to me. It seemed at times, by the circumstances and demands that she contrived, that she was testing the loyalty of my friends—using her own standards, of course—just as she tested her own friends. For example, she insisted that I ask my friends to take care of Kevin or to loan me money. She was in fact teaching me how to get along.

Ruby and I also enjoyed comparing our culturally acquired tastes in furniture and dress. With no intention of buying, we loved to go to the local used furniture store to mock one another's preferences. Ruby admired new, vinyl and Masonite, tough, fake wood modern furniture. I was only interested in finding old turn-of-the-century oak furniture. She laughed at my love for old, used furniture, often warped with age. To her, aged and worn stood for poverty.

Sometimes when Ruby and I were alone we would act out a parody of one another, imitating one another's walk or dancing style, and sometimes this mime would be continued in front of friends. She and I went to white "hilly-billy" taverns not frequented by Blacks with our boyfriends. We dressed "white" in dressy dresses, the men in ties, and we danced the fox-trot to an electric guitar. The reaction to us was silence. People thought we were imitating them. At the next dance, we broke into "black" dance. Ruby and her friends took John* and me to black nightclubs to observe the reaction of their black friends to us. They bought us outfits so we would dress "black." At times the reaction at the clubs was patronizing or even hostile, but Ruby was amused.

Most of our day was spent in The Flats in the company of Ruby's friends and kin. Occasionally, when Ruby and I were with individuals who did not know me or who were apparently hostile, Ruby would cuss, tease, or "signify" to my face. If my response was equally insulting or foul, this would put people at ease. After such a scene Ruby would frequently scold me for not coming up with as good a response as she could have given herself. There is no doubt in my mind that meeting Ruby and gaining an entrée into social relationships in The Flats through her made much of this study possible. Ruby had a quick, affirmative way of letting others know my presence was

---

* John Lombardi, a fellow anthropologist, energetically joined the field study for over two years.

acceptable to her, and that it "damn well better be acceptable to them." At one large family gathering, relatives came from out of town to see Ruby's stepfather, who was sick. Ruby sensed their hostility and insecurity toward me. She turned to me and said, "What is your white ass doing sitting down when there is so much cooking and work to do in my kitchen?" I responded, "My white ass can sit here as long as your black ass can." With that, we both got up, went into the kitchen and got to work.

My mode of transportation varied with the weather. During the first spring and summer of my field work, I walked or rode my bicycle. People in The Flats walk year-round and ride bicycles in good weather. In the process of shopping, visiting, washing clothes, and paying bills, many walk more than five miles a day. Time consumed in walking often involves more than one trip to the same place. If the laundry has been washed, and clothes are ready at the cleaners, and a daily shopping has to be made, one or two or three members of a household, including younger children, may make three or four trips during the day to carry the load of goods home. Walking across town, sharing a work load, carrying packages, riding in a cab, and visiting kin and friends showed me about the pace of life in The Flats and the patience with which the residents endured pain, misfortune, and disappointment. Early in the morning, for example, people in a household might get excited about a large house they heard was for rent or a decent refrigerator that was for sale. A large group of us, including five to ten children, would take a walk to see the house or refrigerator, only to arrive too late.

Picking through piles of clothing at the local Goodwill or at the Salvation Army Store was another frustrating job made even more difficult without a car. Toward the end of the summer many of the women and their children in The Flats began to make daily trips to these second-hand stores, which were located outside The Flats in the Jackson Harbor business district, to pick out enough clothes for all of their children to begin school. For three consecutive summers I spent most of the month of August walking to secondhand stores with families, helping find the right size dresses, shirts, pants, socks, coats, and shoes for their children. The children would look for clothes for themselves and their brothers, sisters, and cousins. They seemed enthusiastic when they found a piece of clothing that would fit someone, but I gained more insight into their real attitude toward these ventures one afternoon when a woman I knew well, Ophelia, asked me to take her eleven-year-old son to Goodwill because "he didn't have a shirt to cover his back." She told us to buy three shirts. Sam and I walked to the store and began the search. We found five shirts his size. Sam seemed pleased. I told him to pick out the three shirts he liked best. He shook his head and said, "Caroline, to tell the truth, I don't like any of them. You pick out three and then let's go show Mama that we got the job done." Sam's response was a mature, resigned response to the necessities of life.

In the fall of 1968 I decided to buy an old car. I thought the car would enable me to visit a variety of people across town while still spending most of the day at my current home base. I thought, too, I could help reduce the tremendous amount of money people spent on cab fare when visiting and shopping, but especially when "carrying" sick children to the doctor or to the hospital in an emergency. I talked it over with Ruby and with others. They all thought it was a fine idea. I had not anticipated some of the disadvantages of acquiring a car.

My car did not substantially increase the flow of goods between people, but it did increase daily visiting and the flow of information between people. For at least two months my role in the community, and in the lives of those people I had become closest to, changed. Before I bought the car I was able to spend most of the day in the company of others, sharing and observing their daily experiences. Once I had the car, people continually asked me to run errands—taking children, goods, and gossip between households. For a while all I seemed to be doing was taking half a pot roast from one house to another, picking up the laundry from a home with a washing machine, going to the liquor store for beer, or waiting with mothers in the local medical clinics for doctors to see their sick children. Although the children of those people often rode around with me, giving me an opportunity to talk to them alone, the intensity of social contact with others was lost. Whenever I would try to spend an afternoon with someone, a new compelling errand had to be run.

As I drove around The Flats, a woman might come up to the car at a stop sign, recognize the children or the adult in the car, and say to me, "You are white Caroline, I heard about you," and then tell my companion to bring me by her home to visit. Often I would drive a companion to her friend's home to borrow or gain back something from a past exchange. I began to observe, firsthand, the content and style of social relationships among residents in The Flats. I also started to observe how residents in The Flats got along with white doctors, dentists, social workers, landlords, shopkeepers, and other residents of Jackson Harbor.

For example, I learned that many of the doctors and medical clinics in the city refuse to make appointments for welfare recipients and their children. Some of those that do do not take the time and interest necessary to improve health. I took one young mother and her sick baby to three different pediatricians. One yelled at the mother for not feeding her baby properly and then quickly scribbled down instructions to a mother who could not read. When the mother took the note to the nurse for help, the nurse scolded her for taking up too much time and for missing a previous appointment. Then the nurse threatened that if this mother missed another appointment, the clinic would never see her babies again.

Also, as I assisted in the search for new housing when people I knew were evicted or were living in condemned houses, I observed the direct confrontation between residents of The Flats and white landlords and social workers. In the two or three months I spent in the process of looking for housing with companions, I saw indifference and racism expressed by the larger white society toward Flats residents. One case history illustrates a typical sequence of events facing a large black family who is forced to move.

In the fall of 1968 Jessie and Eloise, Magnolia's closest friend, and their household, including six children and Jessie's niece, were forced to move after their rented home was condemned. At the time, Jessie was unemployed and Eloise received AFDC benefits for her children. Eloise went to the welfare to tell her case worker that the family would soon be moving. The case worker told Eloise that she was "probably not paying her rent." Eloise was extremely insulted, rode a cab home and returned in a cab to show her case worker rent receipts for the past three years. She told the case worker, "I would be a fool not to pay my rent and have my large family put out on the street."

Eloise, Jessie, their kin and friends looked for housing every day for at least a month and a half. At times, when I was present, we would track down false hopes—houses that appeared to be abandoned, unrented, or available, but were actually inhabited. When Eloise finally found a large house for rent, the landlord wanted several references. Since he had seen me in the company of the family on several occasions, he would not accept my recommendation. Eloise called her social worker and asked her to call the landlord to tell him that she had seen

Eloise's rent receipts for the past three years. The social worker refused and said. "I am not supposed to get involved in anything like that."

After some pressure on the part of Eloise's kin, the social worker did eventually call the landlord. The case worker had "nothing good to say about Eloise." The next day Eloise and I drove to the local welfare office to complain. As we climbed the steps to the welfare building, Eloise said to me, "Here we are where the devils is."

After intense pressure from some white professionals I knew in Jackson Harbor, Eloise got the house. Unfortunately it was condemned soon afterwards, and the search for housing began again.

Despite the fact that my car was a convenience—it gave me an easily explainable role in the lives of the families I knew, helping me provide daily assistance with the children, the shopping, the problems with "papers," the welfare office, sick children, and so on—when it broke down I decided not to fix it. This began a very important stage of the research. Without the car, my presence in the community was less apparent. Once again I was able to spend long days in the homes of people I had met, participating in their daily lives. I had already developed tentative hypotheses on the style of social relations in The Flats and on the ways in which people expand their network of exchange. I began to focus my attention on how networks were expanded, who the participants were, and how residents in The Flats see and interpret this process.

My role in the community at this point was no longer that of an outsider. To many families I became another link in the systems of exchanges that were part of their existence. Viola Jackson's sisters once told me that people look at you when you have a white friend, saying that you are really on the white man's side and that you do everything they want you to do. But Ophelia said to me that people understand what friendship means. Friends can ask any favor of one another, anytime of the night, and it shouldn't make any difference. No one would tell you to drop a friend you can trust even if she is white. Ruby Banks told me that from the first day we started going around together, people said that we looked alike and that we did so much together that we seemed just "like sisters." Our affinity influenced the behavior of Ruby's kin toward me and their persistent concern for my well being. It also influenced Ruby's behavior toward me in public settings within and outside the ghetto. When Ruby's youngest child was sick in the local hospital, we went to visit her. The first day, the white nurse on duty stopped me—the rules stated that only close relatives could visit. Ruby, told the nurse angrily, "Caroline here is my sister, and nothing's stopping her from visiting this baby." Ruby's claim went unchallenged, and we were able to visit the baby every day.

2

BLACK URBAN POOR

STEREOTYPES VERSUS REALITY

Few studies of the black family in the United States have high-lighted either the adaptive strategies, resourcefulness, and re-silience of urban families under conditions of perpetual poverty or the stability of their kin networks. Most of the classic studies of black family life have compared the black family to the white middle-class model. For over fifty years, leading schol-ars of black family life have been content to pigeonhole black culture into preconceived concepts of the mother-father-child (the nuclear model) or the matriarchy (the matrifocal model), hardly questioning their cultural validity.

Despite the stated intentions of scholars, from the thirties and forties (Drake and Cayton 1945; Frazier 1939; Johnson 1941; Myrdal 1944) through the sixties and seventies (Abrahams 1963; Bernard 1966; Hannerz 1969; Keil 1966; Schulz 1969; Banfield 1958), studies tended to reinforce popular stereotypes of the lower class or black family—particularly the black family in poverty—as deviant, matriarchal, and broken. Given the prevailing academic biases, it is not surprising that few attempts have been made to view black families as they actually are, recognizing the interpretations black people have of their own cultural patterns.

Students of black family life have generally ignored the inter-pretations that black people have of their own life experience. Moreover, they have defined the "poverty problem" in the

United States from the point of view of white society, without
regard for the explanations constructed by the poor. The ex-
planatory power of such models is obviously weak, but that they
exist is not surprising. The culture of poverty, as Hylan Lewis
points out, has a fundamental political nature. The idea matters
most to political and scientific groups attempting to rationalize
why some Americans failed to make it in American society. It
is, Lewis (1971) argues, "an idea that people believe, want to
believe, and perhaps need to believe." They want to believe that
raising the income of the poor would not change their life
styles or values, but merely funnel greater sums of money into
bottomless, self-destructing pits. This fatalistic view has wide
acceptance among scholars, welfare planners, and the voting
public. Indeed, even at the most prestigious university, the
country's theories alleging racial inferiority have become in-
creasingly prevalent.

The complex forces that inhibit the poor from changing their
economic situation are in sharp contrast to the explanations
provided by the well-known culture of poverty concept (O.
Lewis 1959, 1966a, 1966b; Harrington 1962).[1] The culture of
poverty notion explains the persistence of poverty in terms of
presumed negative qualities within a culture: family disorganization, group disintegration, personal disorganization, resignation,
and fatalism. An underlying assumption of the culture of
poverty notion is that the social adaptation of the poor to
conditions of poverty would fall apart if these conditions were
altered. It is assumed that the subculture would be left with
no culture, or with wholly negative qualities. But, early on,
Hylan Lewis (1965), then Hannerz (1969), Liebow (1967), and
Valentine (1968) demonstrate that many of the features alleged
to characterize the culture of poverty—unemployment, low
wages, crowded living quarters—are simply definitions of poverty
itself, not of a distinct "culture."

In The Flats, the employment available to those hopeful of

achieving social mobility consists of low-paying, seasonal, and temporary jobs. This is a major factor preventing individuals from breaking out of poverty. In addition, those who attempt social mobility must carefully evaluate their job security, even if it is at poverty level, before they risk removing themselves from the collective help of kinsmen. The collective expectations and obligations created by cooperative networks of poverty-stricken kinsmen in The Flats result in a stability within the kin group, and the success of these networks of kinsmen depends upon this stability.

Recently, many behavioral scientists have attacked racist social science theories like those that have given rise to concepts such as the culture of poverty. In *Blaming the Victim*, William Ryan (1971) dramatically shows the impact of racist thinking on the social sciences and the impact of discrimination on black people. Ryan argues that we cannot blame the victim for his shortcomings. However, even Ryan accepts the social scientists' and policy makers' assumptions by stating that these deviant attributes apply to only a relatively small segment of the black community. He accepts uncritically that poor black families are fatherless families. He believes that stressful events among the poor are followed by unpredictable household changes by adults and children. He concludes (1971, p. 78) that economic stress and discrimination are basic causes of the deterioration of the "Negro" family and that "social pathology and broken homes are twin results." All of these assumptions are challenged in the present book.

Ryan does not ask, for example, what role the ties of kinship or friendship play in the black community, who socializes the children born in the ghetto, what folk criteria qualify a woman to give birth or to raise a child, or what may be the adaptive functions of sexual unions and multiple household kin networks. Because he does not look for the answers to these questions, he must apologize for their life ways.

The recent and vague attack on racism in the behavioral sciences coexists with certain academic support for racial inferiority hypotheses. Going beyond this debate, Valentine (1971), Willhelm (1971), and Piven and Cloward (1971) argue persuasively that the present economic order in the United States is dependent upon cheap labor and economic racism that confines Blacks to low-skilled jobs, low wages, and unsatisfactory employment. Piven and Cloward (1971) argue that relief-giving in America is a supportive institution that serves the larger economic and political order. Piven and Cloward demonstrate the functions of public welfare in their book *Regulating the Poor* (1971, xiii). "Historical evidence," they write, "suggests that relief arrangements are initiated or expanded during the occasional outbreaks of civil disorder produced by mass unemployment, and are then abolished or contracted when political stability is restored."

The nature of the American economy, as explained by Piven and Cloward (1971), requires the poor to devise ways to cope with chronic crisis, catastrophes, and events totally out of their control. Many studies overlook the profound ways that economic and political pressures outside and within the ghetto —the profit motive, the welfare system, the employer, the landlord, the social agency, the school, the physician, the health clinic, the city services—affect cultural patterns, social identity, life chances, and interpersonal relations among the poor. Few studies attempt to recognize the content of the daily life of the poor or the adaptive institutions developed inside the ghetto for coping with poverty.

Many reviews of the literature on the black family demonstrate the failure of social scientists to comprehend the reality of Afro-American culture; see, for example, Gonzalez (1969), *Black Carib Household Structure* (Chapter VI); Whitten and Szwed (1970), *Afro-American Anthropology* (Introduction); Ladner (1971), *Tomorrow's Tomorrow: The Black Woman* (Chapter

I); Valentine (1972), "Black Studies and Anthropology: Scholarly and Political Interests in Afro-American Culture." Little or nothing in the classic works advances our knowledge of how black people organize and interpret their own cultural experience, with the notable exception of the writings of W. E. B. Du Bois, who speaks passionately in *The Souls of Black Folk* (1903) of the "double consciousness"—the conflicting and warring identities between being a Black and an American in a white world. The theme of a black identity and the conflict between racism and the ideology of the American Dream have since been expressed in the writings of many black poets and novelists, and sociologists and psychologists.

This theme has been reinterpreted in political and economic terms in the recent, penetrating writings of Valentine (1972), Willhelm (1971), and Piven and Cloward (1971), and to a lesser extent by Ladner (1971) and Liebow (1967). Hylan Lewis' essays (1965, 1971) and Valentine's early work (1968) challenged the culture of poverty concept (O. Lewis 1959, 1966b) and questioned whether a self-perpetuating culture of poverty exists among poor Blacks. Valentine (1970) raised important political issues, suggesting that the cultural differences in behavior among the poor are structurally imposed by the workings of the stratified, national social-economic system. Between 1968 and 1972 Valentine's explanation of poverty in the United States changed from an apperception of poverty in terms of inequality to a recognition of institutionalized, economic racism. Valentine's study, as a participant, of the material conditions of ghetto life had a decisive effect on his thinking (1970, p. 39). He says, "Participant experience in ghetto existence has brought home to me not only the crushingly determining material conditions of under-class life, but also the integrated economic-ideological functions of all major institutions of the wider society in perpetuating these conditions."

Social scientists have only begun to interpret the impact

of social-economic and service institutions on the Afro-American experience. Joyce Ladner (1971), one of the leaders in this endeavor, in *Tomorrow's Tomorrow* depicts the effects of poverty, discrimination, and institutional subordination on the lives of black adolescent girls in a big-city slum. She sees their response as a healthy, creative adaptation to unhealthy environmental conditions.

The impact of economic oppression on men in the black community is described by Liebow in *Tally's Corner* (1967). His study of the lives of street corner men reveals the psychological effect of "double consciousness" on black men who continue to hold mainstream values even though they are prevented from achievement and employment. Valentine (1970), responding to this issue, identifies the sources of inequality that are external to black culture in the United States and indicates the poignant contrast between the black Americans' commitment to middle-class values and the structural barriers to their attainment of those highly valued goals. His 1970 study of a large, multi-ethnic, but predominantly black, ghetto in the Northeast is the most comprehensive recent study of racial oppression in the United States, a much needed holistic study of urban culture.

AN ANTHROPOLOGICAL APPROACH

In the spring of 1968 I began this study of urban poverty and the "domestic strategies" of urban-born black Americans whose parents had migrated from the South to The Flats. Having just completed a study of patterns of black migration to Northern cities (Stack 1970), I chose to concentrate on family life among second-generation urban dwellers, many of whom were raised on public welfare, and now, as adults in their twenties to forties, are raising their children on welfare (AFDC).[2] I was interested to find out how such families cooperated to produce an adaptive strategy to cope with poverty and racism.

In this study I found extensive networks of kin and friends supporting, reinforcing each other—devising schemes for self-help, strategies for survival in a community of severe economic deprivation. My purpose in this book is to illustrate the collective adaptations to poverty of men, women, and children within the social-cultural network of the urban black family. I became poignantly aware of the alliances of individuals trading and exchanging goods, resources, and the care of children, the intensity of their acts of domestic cooperation, and the exchange of goods and services among these persons, both kin and non-kin. Their social and economic lives were so entwined that not to repay on an exchange meant that someone else's child would not eat. People would tell me, "You have to have help from everybody and anybody," and "The poorer you are, the more likely you are to pay back."

I spent almost three years in The Flats attempting to understand the complexities of their exchange system. I tried to learn how participants in domestic exchanges were defined by one another, what performances and behavior they expected of one another, who was eligible to become a part of the cooperative networks, how they were recruited, and what kept participants actively involved in the series of exchanges. I naturally became involved in these exchanges. If someone asked a favor of me, later I asked a favor of him. If I gave a scarf, a skirt, or a cooking utensil to a woman who admired it, later on when she had something I liked she would usually give it to me. Little by little as I learned the rules of giving and reciprocity, I tried them out.

Eventually the children of those I was closest to would stay overnight or several days at my apartment, and my son stayed at their homes. I found that among kin and friends in The Flats, temporary child-exchange is a symbol of mutual trust. It

provides a means of acquiring self-esteem. People began accept-
ing my trust and respect when I trusted my son with them.

By such informal circulation of children in The Flats, the
poor facilitated the distribution and exchange of the limited
resources available to them. Parental responsibilities toward
children can be shared with the mother and father, or in times
of need, be transferred to others. Throughout the study I
gathered data on the residence patterns of children, "child-
keeping," as they call temporary fosterage, and the circumstances
that require people to raise the children of a friend or kin.

One of my most challenging problems was to assess why
people so readily responded to the pressures to exchange within
kin networks. In the final months of my life in The Flats, I
learned that poverty creates a necessity for this exchange of goods
and services. The needs of families living at bare subsistence are
so large compared to their average daily income that it is impossible for families to provide independently for fixed expenses
and daily needs. Lacking any surplus of funds, they are forced
to use most of their resources for major monthly bills: rent,
utilities, and food. After a family pays these bills they are
penniless.

The poor adopt a variety of tactics in order to survive. They
immerse themselves in a domestic circle of kinfolk who will
help them. To maintain a stable number of people who share
reciprocal obligations, at appropriate stages in the life cycle
people establish socially recognized kin ties. Mothers may
actively seek out their children's father's kin, consciously ex-
panding the number of people who are intimately obligated to
care for one another. It was necessary to examine what counts
as socially recognized parenthood in The Flats—the folk interpretation given to the chain of parent-child connections. This
line of investigation clarified how people acquire socially
recognized kinship relations with others. Friends may be in-
corporated into one's domestic circle: if they satisfy one an-

other's expectations, they may be called kin—cousins, sisters, brothers, daddies.

Those sharing reciprocal obligations toward one another are actively linked participants in an individual's personal kindred. There has been a long, analytical controversy in anthropological literature about how to characterize this web of social relations and obligations. The argument examines whether the kindred is an ego-centered group (Goodenough 1970), a category of relatives having some reciprocal claims and duties (Fox 1967; Keesing 1966), or a category which comes to life for a focal purpose (Fox 1967). In this study, personal kindreds comprise the fully activated, ego-centered network of responsible kin and others defined as kin.

Personal kindreds overlap to form clusters of individuals who can each bring others into the domestic network. Participants in domestic networks in The Flats move quite often and hold loyalties to more than one household grouping at a time. The members of the households to which individuals hold loyalties share mutually conceived domestic responsibilities. Children may be cared for by their parents or by other participants in their parents' domestic network, or they may be transferred back and forth from the household of their mother to the households of other close female kin. The residence patterns of children in The Flats raises questions about the distribution of rights in children, the criteria by which persons are entitled to assume parental roles, and how to define "family" in The Flats.

Traditionally, anthropologists have defined the husband, wife, and their offspring as the basic social-economic unit constituting a family. This unit was regarded as the universal family grouping that provided sexual, economic, and reproductive and educational functions (Murdock 1949). This perspective on the family was clearly inadequate for a study of domestic life in The Flats.

I sought to define the nucleus of familial, social, and eco-

nomic cooperation in The Flats.[3] I gathered multiple interpretations of cultural scenes and events from participants in the
study, and categories emerged that people regarded as relevant
units. As the study progressed, I tried to map out these func-
tional domains of domestic life. It became clear that the
"household" and its group composition was not a meaningful
unit to isolate for analysis of family life in The Flats. A resident in The Flats who eats in one household may sleep in another, and contribute resources to yet another. He may consider
himself a member of all three households.

Ultimately I defined "family" as the smallest, organized,
durable network of kin and non-kin who interact daily, providing domestic needs of children and assuring their survival.
The family network is diffused over several kin-based households, and fluctuations in household composition do not
significantly affect cooperative familial arrangements. The
culturally specific definitions of certain concepts such as family,
kin, parent, and friend that emerged during this study made
much of the subsequent analysis possible. An arbitrary imposi-
tion of widely accepted definitions of the family, the nuclear
family, or the matrifocal family blocks the way to understanding
how people in The Flats describe and order the world in which
they live.

3

SWAPPING

"What Goes Round Comes Round"

Ruby Banks took a cab to visit Virginia Thomas, her baby's aunt, and they swapped some hot corn bread and greens for diapers and milk. In the cab going home Ruby said to me, "I don't believe in putting myself on nobody, but I know I need help every day. You can't get help just by sitting at home, laying around, house-nasty and everything. You got to get up and go out and meet people, because the very day you go out, that first person you meet may be the person that can help you get the things you want. I don't believe in begging, but I believe that people should help one another. I used to wish for lots of things like a living room suite, clothes, nice clothes, stylish clothes—I'm sick of wearing the same pieces. But I can't, I can't help myself because I have my children and I love them and I have my mother and all our kin. Sometimes I don't have a damn dime in my pocket, not a crying penny to get a box of paper diapers, milk, a loaf of bread. But you have to have help from everybody and anybody, so don't turn no one down when they come round for help."

Black families living in The Flats need a steady source of cooperative support to survive. They share with one another because of the urgency of their needs. Alliances between individuals are created around the clock as kin and friends exchange and give and obligate one another. They trade food stamps, rent money, a TV, hats, dice, a car, a nickel here, a cigarette there, food, milk, grits, and children.

Few if any black families living on welfare for the second generation are able to accumulate a surplus of the basic necessities to be able to remove themselves from poverty or from the collective demands of kin. Without the help of kin, fluctuations in the meager flow of available goods could easily destroy a family's ability to survive (Lombardi 1973). Kin and close friends who fall into similar economic crises know that they may share the food, dwelling, and even the few scarce luxuries of those individuals in their kin network. Despite the relatively high cost of rent and food in urban black communities, the collective power within kin-based exchange networks keeps people from going hungry.

As low-skilled workers, the urban poor in The Flats cannot earn sufficient wages and cannot produce goods. Consequently, they cannot legitimately draw desired scarce goods into the community. Welfare benefits which barely provide the necessities of life—a bed, rent, and food—are allocated to households of women and children and are channeled into domestic networks of men, women, and children. All essential resources flow from families into kin networks.

'Whether one's source of income is a welfare check or wages from labor, people in The Flats borrow and trade with others in order to obtain daily necessities. The most important form of distribution and exchange of the limited resources available to the poor in The Flats is by means of trading, or what people usually call "swapping." As people swap, the limited supply of finished material goods in the community is perpetually redistributed among networks of kinsmen and throughout the community.

The resources, possessions, and services exchanged between individuals residing in The Flats are intricately interwoven. People exchange various objects generously: new things, treasured items, furniture, cars, goods that are perishable, and services which are exchanged for child care, residence, or shared meals. Individuals enlarge their web of social relations through repetitive and seemingly habitual instances of swapping. Lily Jones, a resident in The Flats, had this to say about swapping, "That's just everyday life, swapping. You not really getting ahead of nobody, you just get better things as they go back and forth."

THE OBLIGATION TO GIVE

"Trading" in The Flats generally refers to any object or service offered with the intent of obligating. An object given or traded represents a possession, a pledge, a loan, a trust, a bank account—given on the condition that something will be returned, that the giver can draw on the account, and that the initiator of the trade gains prerogatives in taking what he or she needs from the receiver.

Mauss's (1954) classic interpretation of gift exchange in primitive societies stresses the essence of obligation in gift giving, receiving, and repaying. A gift received is not owned and sometimes can be reclaimed by the initiator of the swap. A person who gives something which the receiver needs or desires, gives under a voluntary guise. But the offering is essentially obligatory, and in The Flats, the obligation to repay carries kin and community sanctions.

An individual's reputation as a potential partner in exchange is created by the opinions others have about him (Bailey 1971). Individuals who fail to reciprocate in swapping relationships are judged harshly. Julia Rose, a twenty-five-year-old mother of three, critically evaluated her cousin Mae's reputation, "If someone who takes things from me ain't giving me anything in return, she can't get nothing else. When someone like that, like my cousin Mae, comes to my house and says, 'Ooo, you should give me that chair, honey. I can use it in my living room, and my old man would just love to sit on it,' well, if she's like my cousin, you don't care what her old man wants, you satisfied with what yours wants. Some people like my cousin don't mind borrowing from anybody, but she don't loan you no money, her clothes, nothing. Well, she ain't shit. She don't believe in helping nobody and lots of folks gossip about her. I'll never give her nothing again. One time I went over there after I had given her all these things and I asked her, 'How about loaning me an outfit to wear?' She told me, 'Girl, I ain't got nothing. I ain't got nothing clean. I just put my clothes in the cleaners, and what I do have you can't wear 'cause it's too small for you.' Well, lots of people talks about someone who acts that way."

Degrees of entanglement among kinsmen and friends involved in networks of exchange differ in kind from casual swapping. Those actively involved in domestic networks swap goods and services on a daily, practically an hourly, basis. Ruby Banks, Magnolia Waters' twenty-three-year-old daughter, portrays her powerful sense of obligation to her mother in her words, "She's my mother and I don't want to turn her down." Ruby has a conflicting sense of obligation and of sacrifice toward her mother and her kinsmen.

"I swap back and forth with my mother's family. She wouldn't want nobody else to know how much I'm doing for her, but hell, that's money out of my pocket. We swap back and forth, food stamps, kids, clothes, money, and everything else. Last month the AFDC people had sent me forty dollars to get a couch. Instead of me getting a couch, I took my money over to Mama's and divided with her. I gave her fifteen dollars of it and went on to wash because my kids didn't have a piece clean. I was washing with my hands and a bar of face soap before the money come. I took all the clothes I had, most of the dirty ones I could find, and washed them. It ran me up to six dollars and something with the cab that my sister took back home. I was sitting over at the laundry worrying that Mama didn't have nothing to eat. I took a cab over there and gave her ten more dollars. All I had left to my name was ten dollars to pay on my couch, get food, wash, and everything. But I ignored my problems and gave Mama the money I had. She didn't really have nothing after she paid some bills. She was over there black and blue from not eating—stomach growling. The craziest thing was that she wouldn't touch the rent money. I gave the last five dollars out of the rent money. She paid her sister her five and gave me five to get the kids something to eat. I said, 'What about my other ten?', but she put me off. She paid everybody else and I'm the one who's helping her the most. I could have most everything I needed if I didn't have to divide with my people. But they be just as poor as me, and I don't want to turn them down."

Close kin who have relied upon one another over the years often complain about the sacrifices they have made and the deprivation they have endured for one another. Statements similar to Ruby's were made by men and women describing the sense of obligation and sacrifice they feel toward female kin: their mothers, grandmothers, or "mamas." Commitment to mutual aid among close kin is sometimes characterized as if they were practically "possessed" or controlled by the relationship. Eloise, captured by the incessant demands of her mother, says, "A mother should realize that you have your own life to lead and your own family. You can't come when she calls all the time, although you might want to and feel bad if you can't. I'm all worn out from running from my house to her house like a pinball machine. That's the way I do. I'm doing it 'cause she's my mother and 'cause I don't want to hurt her. Yet, she's killing me."

When Magnolia and Calvin Waters inherited a sum of money, the information spread quickly to every member of their domestic network. Within a month and a half all of the money was absorbed by participants in their network whose demands and needs could not be refused.

The ebb and flow of goods and services among kinsmen is illustrated in the following example of economic and social transactions during one month in 1970 between participants in a kin-based cooperative network in The Flats. As I wrote in my field notes:

Cecil (35) lives in The Flats with his mother Willie Mae, his oldest sister and her two children, and his younger brother. Cecil's younger sister Lily lives with their mother's sister Bessie. Bessie has three children and Lily has two. Cecil and his mother have part-time jobs in a café and Lily's children are on aid. In July of 1970 Cecil and his mother had just put together enough money to cover their rent. Lily paid her utilities, but she did not have enough money to buy food stamps for herself and her children. Cecil and Willie Mae knew that after they paid their rent they would not have any money for food for the family. They helped out Lily by buying her food stamps, and then the two households shared meals together until Willie Mae was paid two weeks later. A week later Lily received her second ADC check and Bessie got some spending money from her boyfriend. They gave some of this money to Cecil and Willie Mae to pay their rent, and gave Willie Mae money to cover her insurance and pay a small sum on a living room suite at the local furniture store. Willie Mae reciprocated later on by buying dresses for Bessie and Lily's daughters and by caring for all the children when Bessie got a temporary job.

The people living in The Flats cannot keep their resources and their needs a secret. Everyone knows who is working, when welfare checks arrive, and when additional resources are available. Members of the middle class in America can cherish privacy concerning their income and resources, but the daily intimacy created by exchange transactions in The Flats insures that any change in a poor family's resources becomes "news." If a participant in an exchange network acquires a new car, new clothes, or a sum of money, this information is immediately circulated through gossip. People are able to calculate on a weekly basis the total sum of money available to their kin network. This information is necessary to their own solvency and stability.

Social relationships between kin who have consistently traded material and cultural support over the years reveal feelings of both generosity and martyrdom. Long-term social interactions, especially between female kin, sometimes become highly competitive and aggressive. At family gatherings or at a family picnic it is not unusual to see an exaggerated performance by someone, bragging about how much he has done for a particular relative, or boasting that he provided all the food and labor for the picnic himself. The performer often combines statements of his generosity with great claims of sacrifice. In the presence of other kin the performer displays loyalty and superiority to others. Even though these routines come to be expected from some individuals, they cause hurt feelings and prolonged arguments. Everyone wants to create the impression that he is generous and manipulative, but no one wants to admit how much he depends upon others.

The trading of goods and services among the poor in complex industrial societies bears a striking resemblance to patterns of exchange organized around reciprocal gift giving in non-Western societies. The famous examples of reciprocal gift giving first described by Malinowski (1922), Mauss (1925), and Lévi-Strauss (1969) provided a basis for comparison. Patterns of exchange among people living in poverty and reciprocal exchanges in cultures lacking a political state are both embedded in well-defined kinship obligations. In each type of social system strategic resources are distributed from a family base to domestic groups, and exchange transactions pervade the whole social-economic life of participants. Neither industrial poor nor participants in nonindustrial economies have the opportunity to control their environment or to acquire a surplus of scarce goods (Dalton 1961; Harris 1971; Lee 1969; Sahlins 1965). In both of these systems a limited supply of goods is perpetually redistributed through the community.

The themes expressed by boasting female performers and gossiping kin and friends resemble themes which have emerged from black myth, fiction, and lore (Abrahams 1963; Dorson 1956, 1958). Conflicting values of trust and distrust, exploitation and friendship, the "trickster" and the "fool," have typically characterized patterns of social interaction between Blacks and Whites; notions of trust and distrust also suffuse interpersonal relations within the black community. These themes become daily utterances between cooperating kinsmen who find themselves trapped in a web of obligations. But the feelings of distrust are more conspicuous among friends than among kin.

Many students of social relations within the black community have concluded that friendships are embedded in an atmosphere of distrust. However, intense exchange behavior would not be possible if distrust predominated over all other attitudes toward personal relations. Distrust is offset by improvisation: an adaptive style of behavior acquired by persons using each situation to control, manipulate, and exploit others. Wherever there are friendships, exploitation possibilities exist (Abrahams 1970b, p. 125). Friends exploit one another in the game of swapping, and they expect to be exploited in return. There is a precarious line between acceptable and unacceptable returns on a swap. Individuals risk trusting others because they want to change their lives. Swapping offers a variety of goods and something to anticipate. Michael Lee, a twenty-eight-year-old Flats resident, talks about his need to trust others, "They say you shouldn't trust nobody, but that's wrong. You have to try to trust somebody, and somebody has to try to trust you, 'cause everybody need help in this world."

A person who gives and obligates a large number of individuals stands a better chance of receiving returns than a person who limits his circle of friends. In addition, repayments from a large number of individuals are returned intermittently: people can anticipate receiving a more-or-less continuous flow of goods. From this perspective, swapping involves both calculation and planning.

Obtaining returns on a trade necessarily takes time. During this process, stable friendships are formed. Individuals attempt to surpass one another's displays of generosity; the extent to which these acts are mutually satisfying determines the duration of friendship bonds. Non-kin who live up to one another's expectations express elaborate vows of friendship and conduct their social relations within the idiom of kinship. Exchange behavior between those friends "going for kin" is identical to exchange behavior between close kin.

THE RHYTHM OF EXCHANGE

"These days you ain't got nothing to be really giving, only to your true friends, but most people trade," Ruby Banks told me. "Trading is a part of everybody's life. When I'm over at a girl friend's house, and I see something I want, I say, 'You gotta give me this; you don't need it no way.' I act the fool with them. If they say no, I need that, then they keep it and give me something else. Whatever I see that I want I usually get. If a friend lets me wear something of theirs, I let them wear something of mine. I even let some of my new clothes out. If my friend has on a new dress that I want, she might tell me to wait till she wear it first and then she'll give it to me, or she might say, well take it on." Exchange transactions are easily formed and create special bonds between friends. They initiate a social relationship and agreed upon reciprocal obligations (Gouldner 1960; Foster 1963; Sahlins 1965).[1]

Reciprocal obligations last as long as both participants are mutually satisfied. Individuals remain involved in exchange relationships by adequately drawing upon the credit they accumulate with others through swapping. Ruby Banks' description of the swapping relationship that developed between us illustrates this notion. "When I first met you, I didn't know you, did I? But I liked what you had on about the second time you seen me, and you gave it to me. All right, that started us swapping back and forth. You ain't really giving nothing away because everything that goes round comes round in my book. It's just like at stores where people give you credit. They have to trust you to pay them back, and if you pay them you can get more things."

Since an object swapped is offered with the intent of obligating the receiver over a period of time, two individuals rarely simultaneously exchange things. Little or no premium is placed upon immediate compensation; time has to pass before a counter-gift or a series of gifts can be repaid. While waiting for repayments, participants in exchange are compelled to trust one another. As the need arises, reciprocity occurs. Opal Jones described the powerful obligation to give that pervades interpersonal relationships. "My girl friend Alice gave me a dress about a ·month ago, and last time I went over to her house, she gave me sheets and towels for the kids, 'cause she knew I needed them. Every time I go over there, she always gives me something. When she comes over to my house, I give her whatever she asks for. We might not see each other in two or three months. But if she comes over after that, and I got something, I give it to her if she want it. If I go over to her house and she got something, I take it—canned goods, food, milk—it don't make no difference.

"My TV's been over to my cousin's house for seven or eight

months now. I had a fine couch that she wanted and I gave it to her too. It don't make no difference with me what it is or what I have. I feel free knowing that I done my part in this world. I don't ever expect nothing back right away, but when I've given something to kin or friend, whenever they think about me they'll bring something on around. Even if we don't see each other for two or three months. Soon enough they'll come around and say, 'Come over my house, I got something to give you.' When I get over there and they say, 'You want this?', if I don't want it my kin will say, 'Well, find something else you like and take it on.' "

When people in The Flats swap goods, a value is placed upon the goods given away, but the value is not determined by the price or market value of the object. Some goods have been acquired through stealing rings, or previous trades, and they cost very little compared to their monetary value. The value of an object given away is based upon its retaining power over the receiver; that is, how much and over how long a time period the giver can expect returns of the gift. The value of commodities in systems of reciprocal gift giving is characterized by Lévi-Strauss (1969, p. 54), "Goods are not only economic commodities, but vehicles and instruments for realities of another order, such as power, influence, sympathy, status and emotion. . . ."

Gifts exchanged through swapping in The Flats are exchanged at irregular intervals, although sometimes the gifts exchanged are of exactly the same kind. Despite the necessity to exchange, on the average no one is significantly better off. Ruby Banks captured the pendulous rhythm of exchange when she said, "You ain't really giving nothing away because everything that goes round comes round in my book."

These cooperating networks share many goals constituting a group identity—goals so interrelated that the gains and losses of any of them are felt by all participants. The folk model of reciprocity is characterized by recognized and urgent reciprocal dependencies and mutual needs. These dependencies are recognized collectively and carry collective sanctions. Members of second-generation welfare families have calculated the risk of giving. As people say, "The poorer you are, the more likely you are to pay back." This criterion often determines which kin and friends are actively recruited into exchange networks.

Gift exchange is a style of interpersonal relationship by which local coalitions of cooperating kinsmen distinguish themselves from other Blacks—those low-income or working-class Blacks who have access to steady employment. In contrast to the middle-class ethic of individualism and competition, the poor living in The Flats do not turn anyone down when they need help. The cooperative life style and the bonds created by the vast mass of moment-to-moment exchanges constitute an underlying element of black identity in The Flats. This powerful obligation to exchange is a profoundly creative adaptation to poverty.

SOCIAL NETWORKS

The most typical way people involve others in their daily domestic lives is by entering with them into an exchange relationship. Through exchange transactions, an individual personally mobilizes others as participants in his social network. Those engaged in reciprocal gift giving are recruited primarily from relatives and from those friends who come to be defined as kin. The process of exchange joins individuals in personal relationships (Boissevain 1966). These interpersonal links effectively define the web of social relationships in The Flats.

Kinsmen and others activated into one another's networks share reciprocal obligations toward one another. They are referred to as "essential kin" in this study.[2] Strings of exchanges which actively link participants in an individual's network define that individual's personal kindred. The personal kindreds described in Chapter 4 are ego-centered networks. Even the personal kindreds of half siblings differ slightly; each half sibling shares some kin, but relates uniquely to others. Personal kindreds are not a category from which individuals are recruited, but a selection of individuals mobilized for specific ends (Goodenough 1970; Keesing 1966).

In the process of exchange, people become immersed in a domestic web of a large number of kinfolk who can be called upon for help and who can bring others into the network. Domestic networks comprise the network of cooperating kinsmen activated from participants' overlapping personal kindreds. Domestic networks are not ego-centered; several participants in the network can recruit kin and friends to participate in domestic exchanges. Similar to personal kindreds, domestic networks are a selection of individuals mobilized for specific ends and they can be mobilized for extended periods of time.

Many descriptions of black American domestic life by both Blacks and Whites (Frazier 1939; Drake and Cayton 1945; Abrahams 1963; Moynihan 1965; Rainwater 1966) have overlooked the interdependence and cooperation of kinsmen in black communities. The underlying assumptions of these studies seem to imply that female-headed households and illegitimacy are symptomatic of broken homes and family disorganization. These studies fail to account for the great variety of domestic strategies in urban black communities. Whitten and Wolfe (1972, p. 41) suggest that one of the advantages of network analysis is that the researcher can avoid mere categorizing of social systems as "disorganized." The network model can explain a particular web of social relations from several points of view. Throughout this study a network perspective is used to interpret the basis of interpersonal links between those individuals mobilized to solve daily domestic problems.

4

PERSONAL KINDREDS

"All Our Kin"

Billy, a young black woman in The Flats, was raised by her mother and her mother's "old man." She has three children of her own by different fathers. Billy says, "Most people kin to me are in this neighborhood, right here in The Flats, but I got people in the South, in Chicago, and in Ohio too. I couldn't tell most of their names and most of them aren't really kinfolk to me. Starting down the street from here, take my father, he ain't my daddy, he's no father to me.[1] I ain't got but one daddy and that's Jason. The one who raised me. My kids' daddies, that's something else, all their daddies' people really take to them—they always doing things and making a fuss about them. We help each other out and that's what kinfolks are all about."

Throughout the world, individuals distinguish kin from non-kin. Moreover, kin terms are frequently extended to non-kin, and social relations among non-kin may be conducted within the idiom of kinship. Individuals acquire socially recognized kinship relations with others through a chain of socially recognized parent-child connections (Goodenough 1970). The chain of parent-child connections is essential to the structuring of kin groups.

Although anthropologists have long recognized the distinction between natural and social parenthood (Malinowski 1930; Radcliffe-Brown 1950; Goodenough 1970; Carroll 1970), until recently most ethnographic data has not clarified those social transactions involving parental rights. This omission has led to the persistent belief that each person is a kinsman of his natural mother and father, who are expected as parents to raise him (Scheffler 1970). Much of the controversial and misleading characterizations of kinship and domestic life can be attributed to this assumption and to the lack of ethnographic data that interprets the meaning people give to the chain of parent-child connections within a particular folk culture.

At birth a child in any society acquires socially recognized kinship relations with others. Who is socially recognized as kin depends largely upon the cultural interpretation of the chain of parent-child connections. Young black children in The Flats are born into personal networks that include some "essential kin,"[2] those people who actively accept responsibility toward them, and some "relatives" who do not actively create reciprocal obligations.

My experience in The Flats suggests that the folk system of parental rights and duties determines who is eligible to be a member of the personal kinship network of a newborn child. This system of rights and duties should not be confused with the official, written statutory law of the state. The local, folk system of rights and duties pertaining to parenthood are enforced only by sanctions within the community. Community members clearly operate within two different systems: the folk system and the legal system of the courts and welfare offices.[3]

MOTHERHOOD

Men and women in The Flats regard child-begetting and childbearing as a natural and highly desirable phenomenon. Lottie James was fifteen when she became pregnant. The baby's father, Herman, the socially recognized genitor, was a neighbor and the father of two other children. Lottie talked with her mother during her second month of pregnancy. She said, "Herman went and told my mama I was pregnant. She was in the kitchen cooking. I told him not to tell nobody, I wanted to keep it a secret, but he told me times will tell. My mama said to me, 'I had you and you should have your child. I didn't get rid of you. I loved you and I took care of you until you got to the age to have this one. Have your baby no matter what, there's nothing wrong with having a baby. Be proud of it like I was proud of you.' My mama didn't tear me down; she was about the best mother a person ever had."

Unlike many other societies, black women in The Flats feel few if any restrictions about childbearing. Unmarried black women, young and old, are eligible to bear children, and frequently women bearing their first children are quite young.

A girl who gives birth as a teen-ager frequently does not raise and nurture her firstborn child. While she may share the same room and household with her baby, her mother, her mother's sister, or her older sister will care for the child and become the child's "mama." This same young woman may actively become a "mama" to a second child she gives birth to a year or two later. When, for example, a grandmother, aunt, or great-aunt "takes a child" from his natural mother, acquired parenthood often lasts throughout the child's lifetime. Although a child kept by a close female relative knows who his mother is, his "mama" is the woman who "raised him up." Young mothers and their firstborn daughters are often raised as sisters, and lasting ties are established between these mothers and their daughters. A child being raised by his grandmother may later become playmates with his half siblings who are his age, but he does not share the same claims and duties and affective ties toward his natural mother.

A young mother is not necessarily considered emotionally ready to nurture a child; for example, a grandmother and other close relatives of Clover Greer, Viola Jackson's neighbor, decided that Clover was not carrying out her parental duties. Nineteen when her first child, Christine, was born, Clover explains, "I really was wild in those days, out on the town all hours of the night, and every night and weekend I layed my girl on my mother. I wasn't living home at the time, but Mama kept Christine most of the time. One day Mama up and said I was making a fool of her, and she was going to take my child and raise her right. She said I was immature and that I had no business being a mother the way I was acting. All my mama's people agreed, and there was nothing I could do. So Mama took my child. Christine is six years old now. About a year ago I got married to Gus and we wanted to take Christine back. My baby, Earl, was living with us anyway. Mama blew up and told everyone how I was doing her. She dragged my name in the mud and people talked so much it really hurt." Gossip and pressure from close kin and friends made it possible for the grandmother to exercise her grandparental right to take the child into her home and raise her there.

In the eyes of the community, a young mother who does not perform her duties has not validated her claim to parenthood. The person who actively becomes the "mama" acquires the major cluster of parental rights accorded to the mothers in The Flats. In effect, a young mother transfers some of her claims to motherhood without surrendering all of her rights to the child.

Nothing in the conception of parenthood among people in The Flats prevents kinsmen of a child's socially recognized parents from having claims to parenthood (Goodenough 1970, p. 17). Kinsmen anticipate the help they may have to give to young mothers and the parental responsibilities they may have to assume toward the children of kinsmen. The bond between mothers and children is exceedingly strong, and the majority of mothers in The Flats raise their own children. Statistical data on residence patterns and kin relationships of 1,000 AFDC children in Jackson County was gathered from AFDC case histories (see Appendix B). Of the 188 AFDC mothers surveyed, 30 percent were raising their own children, 5 percent were raising younger siblings, and 7 percent were raising their grandchildren, nieces, or nephews.

Just how a "mama" provides a child with concerned relatives can best be viewed in terms of Fischer's (1958) notion of sponsorship.[4] Fischer, in his discussion of residence, calls attention to the question of who is an individual's immediate sponsor in a residence group. This term refers to the sponsorship of individuals rather than of couples, a flexible means of providing· information on residence over an individual's lifetime. The term can also be applied to the creation of personal kinship networks for the newborn child. Determining who becomes one of the immediate sponsors of a child's network clarifies its initial formation, the kinship links that are effective, and the shape of the network.

In The Flats the recognized mother, the "mama" (80 percent are the natural mothers), determines the child's kinship affiliations through females. She is one of the immediate sponsors of a child's personal kinship network. A black child's "mama's" relatives and their husbands and wives are eligible to be members of the child's personal kinship network. How the relationship between a child's natural mother and his or her socially recognized genitor determines a child's kin affiliations through males is described below. When a child is raised by close female relatives of his mother in a more-or-less stable situation, the immediate sponsor of the child's personal network is the "mama." This reckoning of relatives through the immediate sponsor is especially useful when a child's residence changes during his lifetime. Even if a child is raised by a person who is not a blood relative (described below), he usually becomes a part of the network of his "mama."

FATHERHOOD

People in The Flats expect to change friends frequently through a series of encounters. Demands on friendships are great, but social-economic pressures on male-female relationships are even greater. Therefore, relationships between young, unmarried, childbearing adults are highly unstable. Some men and childbearing women in The Flats establish long-term liaisons with one another, some maintain sexual unions with more than one person at a time, and still others get married. However, very few women in The Flats are married before they have given birth to one or more children. When a man and woman have a sexual partnership, especially if the woman has no other on-going sexual relationships, the man is identified with children born to the woman. Short-term sexual partnerships are recognized by the community even if a man and woman do not share a household and domestic responsibilities. The offspring of these unions are publicly accepted by the community; a child's existence seems to legitimize the child in the eyes of the community.

But the fact of birth does not provide a child with a chain of socially recognized relatives through his father. Even though the community accepts the child, the culturally significant issue in terms of the economics of everyday life is whether any man involved in a sexual relationship with a woman provides a newborn child with kinship affiliations. A child is eligible to participate in the personal kinship network of his father if the father becomes an immediate sponsor of a child's kinship network.

When an unmarried woman in The Flats becomes pregnant or gives birth to a child, she often tells her friends and kin who the father is. The man has a number of alternatives open to him. Sometimes he publicly denies paternity by implying to his friends and kin that the father could be any number of other men, and that he had "information that she is no good and has been creeping on him all along." The community generally accepts the man's denial of paternity. It is doubtful that under these conditions this man and his kin would assume any parental duties anyway. The man's failure to assent to being the father leaves the child without recognized kinship ties through a male. Subsequent "boyfriends" of the mother may assume the paternal duties of discipline and support and receive the child's affection, but all paternal rights in the child belong to the mother and her kinsmen. The pattern whereby black children derive all their kin through females has been stereotyped and exaggerated in the literature on black families. In fact, fathers in The Flats openly recognized 484 (69 percent) of 700 children included in my AFDC survey.

The second alternative open to a man involved in a sexual relationship with a mother is to acknowledge openly that he is responsible. The father can acknowledge the child by saying "he own it," by telling his people and his friends that he is the father, by paying part of the hospital bill, or by bringing milk and diapers to the mother after the birth of the child. The parents may not have ever shared a household and the affective and sexual relationship between them may have ended before the birth of the child.

The more a father and his kin help a mother and her child, the more completely they validate their parental rights. However, since many black American males have little or no access to steady and productive employment, they are rarely able to support and maintain their families. This has made it practically impossible for most poor black males to assume financial duties as parents. People in The Flats believe a father should help his child, but they know that a mother cannot count on his help. But, the community expects a father's kin to help out. The black male who does not actively become a "daddy," but acknowledges a child and offers his kin to that child, in effect, is validating his rights. Often it is the father's kin who activate the claim to rights in the child.

Fatherhood, then, belongs to the presumed genitor if he, or others for him, choose to validate his claim. Kinship through males is reckoned through a chain of social recognition. If the father fails to do anything beyond merely acknowledging the child, he surrenders most of his rights, and this claim can be shared or transferred to the father's kin, whose claim becomes strengthened if they actively participate as essential kin. By failing to perform parental duties the father retains practically no rights in his child, although his kin retain rights if they assume active responsibility.

By validating his claim as a parent the father offers the child his blood relatives and their husbands and wives as the child's kin—an inheritance so to speak. As long as the father acknowledges his parental entitlement, his relatives, especially his mother and sisters, consider themselves kin to the child and therefore responsible for him. Even when the mother "takes up with another man," her child retains the original set of kin gained through the father who sponsored him.

A nonparticipating father also shares some of his rights and duties with his child's mother's current boyfriend or husband. When a man and woman have a continuing sexual relationship, even if the man is not the father of any of the woman's children, he is expected by the mother and the community to share some of the parental duties of discipline, support, and affection.

A child's father's kin play an active role in the nurturing of children, and as a result they have the right to observe and judge whether a woman is performing her duties as a mother. If a young woman is unable to care for her child, nothing prevents a father's close female relatives from claiming parental rights. When 188 AFDC mothers listed in order of rank who they would expect to raise each of their children (total of 1,000 children) if they died, one-third of the women listed their own mother as their first choice and one-third listed either their child's father or the father's mother as the first choice. The remaining one-third (second through fifth choice) were close kin to the mother (her mother's sister, her own sister or brother, and her daughter). In crisis situations, such as a mother's death or sickness, a child's kin through his mother and father are equally eligible to assume responsibilities of jural parenthood.

The chain of sponsored parent-child connections determines the personal kindreds of children. Participants in active units of domestic cooperation are drawn from personal kinship networks. How a particular individual, say a mother, works to create the active networks which she depends upon for the needs of her children, depends largely on sponsorship or parental links. Commonly, the mother's personal domestic network includes the personal networks of her children, who are half siblings with different fathers. Each child will grow up into a slightly different personal network from his brothers and sisters. Mothers expect little from the father; they just hope that he will help out. But they do expect something from his kin, especially his mother and sisters. Mothers continually activate these kin lines, and since the biological father's female relatives are usually poor, they too try to expand their network. The exchanges and daily dependencies get very complicated, but they constitute the main activity of daily life for these women.

Daily life is also complicated as individuals expand their own personal networks, in part by recruiting friends into their own domestic networks. When friends live up to one another's expectations, they are identified as kin. Friends often participate in the personal networks of others within the idiom of kinship, and some kin exhibit the interactive patterns of friends.

Domestic arrangements and strategies among the black poor

in The Flats usually assure that children are cared for and that kin and friends in need will be helped. Participants in cooperative networks are primarily drawn from personal kindreds. R. T. Smith (1970, p. 68) has stated that although there is a tendency among "lower classes" to keep kin links open, this does not mean that large cooperating groups of kinsmen are found among the "lower classes." But I found, to the contrary, stable domestic networks of cooperating kinsmen among the poorest black people. These kinship networks have stability because the needs of the poor are constant. Friendships, on the other hand, change more often, and friends drop in and out of one another's networks while assuming a stable position in their own kinship network. From the individual's viewpoint, he is immersed in a domestic circle in which he can find help (Stack 1970).

Similar to patterns found in The Flats, American middle-class children are born into a network of relatives which in principle is infinite. Relatives on both sides of the family are kin, and there is no clear-cut limit to the range of one's kinsmen. But cognatic reckoning by itself cannot distinguish between essential kin and others within the system.[5] The choice of which relatives an individual draws into her personal kindred is by no means mechanical.

How individuals cast their net to create personal kinship networks depends upon the culturally determined perceptions of jural parenthood: the rules and criteria for including and excluding persons connected by blood and marriage to a particular kinsman, and the interpersonal relations between these individuals. These criteria determine which individuals acquire socially recognized kinship relations with others.[6]

Personal kindreds of adults are ego-centered networks of essential kin. These networks are not residential units or observable groups, and they change participants, for example, when friends "fall out" with one another. From the individual's viewpoint personal kindreds comprise the people who are socially recognized as having reciprocal responsibilities. These people become acting and reacting participants for some focal purpose (Fox 1967, p. 167).

Young children exercise little choice in determining with whom they have kinship relations. They are born into a network of essential kin which is primarily the personal kindred of the kinfolk responsible for them. As children become adults they expand, contract, and create their own personal networks.

Geographical distance, interpersonal relations, or acknowledgment of paternity discourage some relatives from actuating claims of responsibility. These relatives effectively drop out of the individual's personal kinship network, and all of the people linked through them also tend to drop out. Thus, an important criterion affecting the size and shape of the personal kinship network of adults is whether the relative who drops out of the network is genealogically close or distant. Sometimes close kinship links, like that of a parent, are broken. A father, for example, may claim that he doesn't "own the baby," thereby refusing to acknowledge paternity. When a close link such as that of a father is broken, it has a profound effect on the shape of the personal kindred.

The following chart shows the genealogical categories in American kinship (consider the "child" as EGO). If a child's grandparents through his father, for example, break a link, all those individuals related through the grandparents effectively drop out of the child's personal kinship network. Chart B shows the shape of a network in which a father has broken a kinship link.

Because any relative can break a link, personal kindreds can take any number of shapes. But the networks are skewed roughly in proportion to the nearness of the kinship links which are ineffective. In principle, the dropping of a father from a network affects the shape of the network in the same way as if

CHART A: <u>GRANDPARENTAL LINK BROKEN</u>

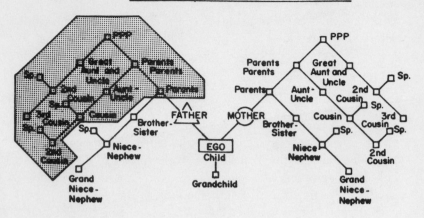

CHART B: <u>PARENTAL LINK BROKEN</u>

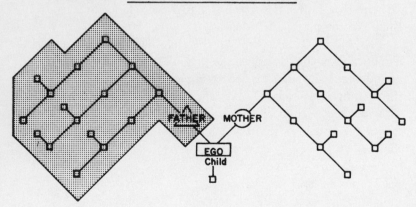

other more distant relatives on either side were to drop out. But the effect of dropping a close relative is obviously much more profound.

FRIENDSHIP

Men and women in The Flats know that the minimal funds they receive from low-paying jobs on welfare do not cover their monthly necessities of life: rent, food, and clothing. They must search for solutions in order to survive. They place their hopes in the scene of their life and action: in the closed community, in the people around them, in kin and friends, and in the new friends they will make to get along. Friendships between lovers and between friends are based upon a precarious balance of trust and profit. Magnolia describes this balance, "I don't have nothing great and no more than nobody else. It doesn't matter. I'm happy with my kids and I'm happy with the friends that I got. Some people don't understand friendship. Friendship means a lot, that is if you can trust a friend. If you have a friend, you should learn to trust them and share everything that you have. When I have a friend and I need something, I don't ask, they just automatically tell me that they going to give it to me. I don't have to ask. And that's the way friends should be, for how long it lasts. But sometimes when you help a person they end up making a fool out of you. If a friend ain't giving me anything in return for what I'm giving her, shit, she can't get nothing else. These days you ain't got nothing to be really giving. You can't care for no one that don't give a damn for you."

Even in newly formed friendships, individuals begin to rely upon one another quickly, expecting wider solutions to their problems than any one person in the same situation could possibly offer. As a result the stability of a friendship often depends upon the ability of two individuals to gauge their

exploitation of one another. Everyone understands that friendships are explosive and abruptly come to an end when one
friend makes a fool out of another. Life, therefore, as Abrahams
shows, is "conceived of in terms of a series of encounters with
a large number of individuals" (1970, p. 120). As Ruby says,
"You got to go out and meet people, because the very day you
go out, that first person you meet may be the person that can
help you get the things you want."

Individuals in The Flats continually evaluate their friendships by gossip and conversation. They talk about whether
others are "acting right" or "doing right by them." They define personal relationships in terms of their dual expectations
of friends and kin. When friends more than adequately share
the exchange of goods and services, they are called kinsmen.
When friends live up to one another's expectations, their social
relations are conducted as kin. For example, if two women of
the same age are helping one another, they call their friend
"just a sister," or say that "they are going for sisters." Anyone
in the community with whom a person has good social dealings
can be classified as some kind of kin. When a friendship ends
because individuals "let one another down," this concludes both
their expectations of one another and their kin relationship.
In addition, a person defined as a kin, for example, a "sister,"
does not usually bring to the relationship her own personal
genealogical entailments. Her mother is not necessarily her
"sister's" mother and her father's father is not her "sister's"
grandfather. Losing a fictive relative, therefore, does not
dramatically affect the shape of personal networks as does the
dropping of a close kinship link.

The offering of kin terms to "those you count on" is a way
people expand their personal networks. A friend who is classified as a kinsman is simultaneously given respect and responsibility.

When a mother has a boyfriend, the community expects

that he will assume some parental duties toward her children. This is especially true if the couple are "housekeeping," sharing their domestic tasks. A father surrenders many of his rights and responsibilities to the mother's husband or current boyfriend. The attitude and behavior of the boyfriend toward the children defines his relationship to them. Clover compares her last two boyfriends and how they dealt with her children. "I stopped going with Max because he took no time for my kids; he just wanted them out of our way. I took it for a while, 'cause I got things from him, but when he hit my boy I called it quits. If he can't care, he can't bully my kids. But Lee, he was something else. He was so nice to my kids that the babies cried when he left the house. Sometimes I had to yell to keep the kids from bothering him and get some time for myself. After we was housekeeping for about six months, Lee said to the boys that they should call him their 'play daddy.' Lee and I quit last year and I'm sorry we did, 'cause the kids really miss him. But he still comes over, especially when I'm out, and they still call him their 'play daddy.' "

Fictive kin relations are maintained by consensus between individuals, and in some contexts can last a lifetime. If Lee maintains his interest in Clover's boys, he may remain their "play daddy" throughout their adult life.

Children very often establish close and affectionate ties with their aunts and uncles, for example, with their mother's sister's "old man" and their mother's brother's "old lady." These aunts and uncles, on the basis of their original consensual relationship, can remain in a child's personal network for a long time. Personal kinship networks are enlarged by the inclusion of these affines who may keep the relationship active. Ruby recently visited her Uncle Arthur, one of her Aunt Augusta's "old men," in the hospital. "Uncle Arthur and I was always good friends," says Ruby, "even when he and Aunt Augusta weren't getting on. He was staying with Augusta, my grandmother, and me when I was just a kid, and he always treated me like something real special. Now he is just as nice to my kids when he comes over to see them. I really feel sad that he's old and sick; he has high blood, and I think he may die." Ruby is also attached to her Uncle Lazar, who started going with her mother's youngest sister when her aunt was just fifteen. "My aunt has been married twice since, but Uncle Lazar just remained a part of our family. He's fifty-eight now and he's been a part of our family ever since I can remember. He always has been staying with our family too. Right now he's staying in the basement below Aunt Augusta's apartment and she cooks for him and her old man. He'll always be my uncle and he and my aunt never did get married."

Just as these "aunts" and "uncles" remain in the personal kinship networks of their nieces and nephews, best friends may remain in each other's domestic network on the basis of original friendship even if the friendship has ended. Sometimes when non-kin become a part of a family and are given a fictive kin term, no one remembers just how the tie began. Billy tried to remember how cousin Ola became a part of her family. "My mama once told me," said Billy, "but I hardly remember. I think cousin Ola was my mama's oldest sister's best friend and they went for cousins. When my mama's sister died, Ola took her two youngest children, and she has been raising them up ever since."

In the above examples, social relations are conducted within the idiom of kinship. Members of the community explain the behavior of those around them by allowing behavior to define the nature of the relationship. Friends are classified as kinsmen when they assume recognized responsibilities of kinsmen. Those kin who cannot be counted upon are severely criticized. Harsh evaluation of the behavior of others accounts for some of the constant ups and downs in the lives of friends and kin. Expectations are so elastic that when one person fails to meet another's needs, disappointment is cushioned. Flexible expectations and the extension of kin relationships to non-kin allow for the creation of mutual aid domestic networks which are not bounded by genealogical distance or genealogical criteria. Much more important for the creation and recruitment to personal networks are the practical requirements that kin and friends live near one another.

Members of domestic networks in The Flats are drawn from kin and friends. Of the two, the kin network is more enduring because all of an individual's essential kin are "recognized as having some duties toward him and some claims on him" (Fox 1967, p. 167). Friendships end and that is to be expected; new friendships can be formed. But the number of relatives who can be called upon for help from personal kinship networks is limited. As a result a cluster of relatives from personal kinship networks have continuing claims on one another. Some observers of daily life in black communities regard the friendship network as the "proven and adaptive base of operations" in lower-class life (Abrahams 1970, p. 128). But the adaptive base of operations of the poorest black people can be attributed to personal kindreds as well as to networks of friends.

5

CHILD-KEEPING

"Gimme a Little Sugar"

The black community has long recognized the problems and difficulties that all mothers in poverty share. Shared parental responsibility among kin has been the response. The families I knew in The Flats told me of many circumstances that required co-resident kinsmen to take care of one another's children or situations that required children to stay in a household that did not include their biological parents.

Most of the adults involved in this study had been fostered at one time or another by kinsmen. Some of their own children are currently residing in the homes of kinsmen, or have been kept by kinsmen in the past. These alternatives enable parents to cope with poverty; they are possibilities that every mother understands.

People in The Flats often regard child-keeping[1] as part of the flux and elasticity of residence. The expansion and contraction of households, and the successive recombinations of kinsmen residing together, require adults to care for the children residing in their household. As households shift, rights and responsibilities with regard to children are shared. Those women and men who temporarily assume the kinship obligation to care for a child, fostering the child indefinitely, acquire the major cluster of rights and duties ideally associated with "parenthood."

Within a network of cooperating kinsmen, there may be

three or more adults with whom, in turn, a child resides. In this cycle of residence changes, the size of the dwelling, employment, and many other factors determine where children sleep. Although patterns of eating, visiting, and child care may bring mothers and their children together for most of the day, the adults immediately responsible for a child change with the child's residence. The residence patterns of children in The Flats have structural implications for both the ways in which rights in children distribute socially and also the criteria by which persons are entitled to parental roles.

From the point of view of the children, there may be a number of women who act as "mothers" toward them; some just slightly older than the children themselves. A woman who intermittently raises a sister's or a niece's or a cousin's child regards their offspring as much her grandchildren as children born to her own son and daughter.

The number of people who can assume appropriate behaviors ideally associated with parental and grandparental roles is increased to include close kinsmen and friends. Consequently, the kin terms "mother," "father," "grandmother," and the like are not necessarily appropriate labels for describing the social roles. Children may retain ties with their parents and siblings and at the same time establish comparable relationships with other kinsmen. There is even a larger number of friends and relatives who may request a hug and kiss, "a little sugar," from children they watch grow up. But they do not consistently assume parental roles toward those children. Parental role behavior is a composite of many behavior patterns (Keesing 1969) and these rights and duties can be shared or transferred to other individuals.

Natural processes and events in the life cycle create new child-care needs and new household alignments. It is not uncommon for young children residing in the homes of rather aging kin who become too old to care for them to be shifted to another kinsmen's home. At these times, the fostering parent often decides who is next in line to raise the child.

Loretta Smart, a forty-year-old Flats resident was raised by her great-grandfather for the first five years of her life. "When I became five years old," Loretta told me, "my daddy just got too old to care for me. My mother was living in The Flats at the time, but my daddy asked my mother's brother and his wife to take me 'cause he really trusted them with me. I stayed with them and their three kids, but my mother came by and took care of us kids lots of times. When I was about nine years old my mother got married and from then on I stayed with her and her husband and he gave me his name."

Close kin may fully cooperate in child care and domestic activities during times when they do not live together. On the other hand, kin may actively assume a parental right in children, insisting upon joining a household in order to help in child care. Amanda Johnson's mother had a hard time keeping track of her three daughters even when they were pretty young. "My grandmother decided to move in with us to bring us up right. She was old then, on a small pension, and getting some help from her son. She stayed for about four years, but she and my mother didn't get on. They fought a lot. After my grandmother died, all our kin in The Flats was helping us out and we didn't want for nothing. One of my uncles kept us and fed us every Thursday and Sunday night when my mother worked, and another uncle got us all our clothing. We was really being kept good."

For many of the families I knew in The Flats, there were circumstances that required mothers and fathers to sleep in households apart from their children. A close look at the housing of children in homes that do not include their biological parents shows how misleading it is to regard child-keeping apart from residence patterns, alliances, and the interpersonal relationships of adults, and from the daily exchanges between kinsmen in the domestic network of the child.

The beginning of a new relationship between a man and woman, or the end of a marriage or consensual union, may cause a family to temporarily separate. Geraldine Penney left her husband because she was told that he had been "fooling around." "After that," she told me, "my family was really split in parts for a while. I sent my three oldest children to stay with my husband's aunt (husband's mother's sister), my middle girl stayed downstairs with my husband's mother, and my two youngest stayed here with my mother."

When a woman enters a new marriage or consensual relationship, occasionally she temporarily disperses her children among kin (Goody 1966; Midgett 1969). Soon after Flats resident Henrietta Davis returned to The Flats to take care of her own children, she told me, "My old man wanted me to leave town with him and get married. But he didn't want to take my three children. I stayed with him for about two years and my children stayed in town with my mother. Then she told me to come back and get them. I came back and I stayed."

Occasionally adolescents decide on their own that they want to live with a kinsmen other than the one with whom they are residing, and they have that option open to them. Boys, for example, who have maintained a close relationship with their natural father may choose to go and live with him. Bernard Smith said that his father started buying him clothes when he was half grown. When Bernard was sixteen he decided to go and stay with his father because "he lived near the center of town." Bernard is twenty-five now, and even though he visits his mother nearly twice a week, he is still living with his father.

When a young girl becomes pregnant, the closest adult female kin of the girl, or of the unborn child, is expected to assume partial responsibility for the young child. Usually rights in such children are shared between the mother and appropriate female kin. If the mother is extremely young, she may "give the child" to someone who wants the child—for example, to the child's father's kin, to a childless couple, or to close friends. Lily Proctor ran away from home in Mississippi when she was fourteen. She ran off to Chicago and then went to The Flats. The friends of kin from the South who took her in had two sons. She gave birth to the oldest boy's baby, but, Lily recalls, "I was in no way ready for a baby. The baby's grandmother [father's mother] wanted the baby, so I gave my baby to her and she adopted her as her own."

Children are sometimes given to non-kin who express love, concern, and a desire to keep a child. Oliver Lucas, a thirty-year-old Flats resident lives with his mother and his sister and her children. Oliver and his kin have been raising his girl friend's child since she was a baby. "My girl friend had six children when I started going with her, but her baby daughter was really something else. I got so attached to that baby over about two years that when my girl friend and I quit, I asked if she would give the baby to me. She said fine, and my 'daughter' has been living with me, my mother, my grandmother, my sisters and brothers ever since. My daughter is ten years old now. She sees her mother now and then, and her father takes her to church with him sometimes, but our family is really the only family she's ever had."

Bonds of obligation, alliance, and dependence among kinsmen are created and strengthened in a variety of ways. Goods and services are the main currency exchanged among cooperating kinsmen. Children too may be transferred back and forth, "borrowed" or "loaned." It is not uncommon for individuals to talk about their residence away from their mother as a fact over which she had little or no control. For example, kin may insist upon "taking" a child to help out. Betty Simpson's story repeats itself with her own daughter. "My mother already had three children when I was born. She had been raised by her maternal great-aunt. After I was born my mother's great-aunt insisted on taking me to help my mother out. I stayed there after my mother got married and moved to The Flats. I wanted to move there too, but my 'mama' didn't want to give me up and my mother didn't want to fight with her. When I was fourteen I left anyway and my mother took me in. When my youngest daughter got polio my mother insisted on taking her. I got a job and lived nearby with my son. My mother raised my little girl until my girl died."

A mother may request or require kin to keep one of her children. An offer to keep the child of a kinsman has a variety of implications for child givers and receivers. It may be that the mother has come upon hard times and desperately wants her close kinsmen to temporarily assume responsibility for her children. Kinsmen rarely refuse such requests to keep one another's children. Likewise they recognize the right of kin to request children to raise away from their own parents (Goody 1966). Individuals allow kinsmen to create alliances and obligations toward one another, obligations which may be called upon in the future.

It might appear that the events described above contribute to a rather random relocation of individuals in dwellings, and a random distribution of the rights individuals acquire in children. But this is not the case. Individuals constantly face the reality that they may need the help of kin for themselves and their children. As a result they anticipate these needs, and from year to year they have a very clear notion of which kinsmen would be willing to help. Their appraisal is simple because it is an outcome of calculated exchanges of goods and services between kinsmen. Consequently, residence patterns and the dispersing of children in households of kin are not haphazard.

STATISTICAL PATTERNS

The responsibility of caring for children in The Flats is a kin obligation. It is not necessarily a role required of a single individual. Rights in children are delegated to kin who are participants in domestic networks of cooperation. In 1970 four-fifths of the children in The Flats were being raised by their mothers. One-fifth of the children were living with kinsmen rather than with their mothers.

TABLE 1

Frequency of Child-Keeping, AFDC Data

	FREQUENCY	PERCENTAGE
Children raised by biological mother	559	81
Children raised by adult female kin	127	18
Children raised by non-kin	8	1
	694	100

Information on the frequency of fosterage collected from AFDC case histories in Jackson County shows that one-fifth of 694 dependent children were assigned to the welfare grant of a close female kinsman other than their mother. This means that the adult female responsible for the child is not the child's mother. Table 2 shows the frequency of fostering based upon AFDC case histories and the relationship of grantees to AFDC children on their grant and in their households.

These statistics on the frequency of fostering are in fact much lower than actual instances of child-keeping in The Flats. According to the AFDC case histories, 81 percent of the dependent childern are being raised by their own mothers, and 18 percent by close female kinsmen. Grantees must claim that a dependent child is residing in their household in order to

TABLE 2

Frequency of Child-Keeping, AFDC Data

	FREQUENCY	TOTAL	PERCENTAGE
Children raised by			
biological mother	559	559	81
Children raised by			
adult female kin:			
younger sibling	34		
sibling's child	34		
grandchild	24		
other kin	35	127	18
Non-kin	8	8	1
		694	100

receive benefits for the child. But my personal contact with individuals whose case histories make up the statistical survey clearly shows disagreement between the record and actual residence patterns. Mothers temporarily shift the residence of their children in response to changes in their own personal relationships, or because of illness or pregnancy or housing problems. Dependent children, and the funds for these children, are dispersed into households of cooperating kinsmen. In the process of switching the residence of children, mothers or grantees rarely report these residence changes to the welfare office.

The variance between the statistics and actual residence patterns is also demonstrated in detailed life histories of adults and children involved in the study. The residential life histories[2] of children show that at least one-third of the children have been "kept" by kinsmen one or two times during their childhood. Consequently the frequency of child-keeping in The Flats is higher than the AFDC statistics indicate. The lower limit of child-keeping in The Flats may be 20 percent, but the range of child-keeping is between 20 percent and 35 percent.

Important factors which show the relationship between patterns of child-keeping and the daily domestic organization of cooperating kinsmen are the age, status, and geographical location of the mothers of dependent children assigned to grantees who are not the child's mother. Field observations of 139 dependent children who are assigned to a grantee other than their mother revealed that practically one-half of those children's mothers generally resided in the same dwelling as their child. Many of those mothers were teen-agers when their first child was born. At the time of the survey only 6 percent of them were under eighteen. Table 3 shows the status and location of biological mothers whose dependent children were assigned to AFDC grants of female kinsmen. According to the female kin now responsible for the children (Table 3), only 8 percent of the mothers had actually deserted their children. Three-fourths of

TABLE 3

Status and Location of Biological Mother

STATUS AND LOCATION OF BIOLOGICAL MOTHER	FREQUENCY	PERCENTAGE
Married adult (over 18)		
Resides in grantee's house	34	24
Adult		
Lives in The Flats	34	24
Unmarried adult		
Resides in grantee's house	19	14
Mother deserted child	11	8
Married or unmarried minor		
Resides in grantee's house	9	6
Not ascertainable	32	24

the biological mothers of these children were living in The Flats at the time of the survey. They resided intermittently in the grantee's household, the household of a kinsman, or from time to time in a separate residence with male or female friends.

The examples above point to the confusion that can arise when statistical data is interpreted out of context. Statistical patterns do not divulge underlying cultural patterns. This confusion between statistics and cultural patterns underlies most interpretations of black family life.

Another clear example of this confusion is the assumption discussed earlier that black children derive all their jural kin through females. Widely popularized statistics on female-headed households have contributed to the classification of black households as matrifocal or matriarchal and to the assumption that black children derive nothing of sociological importance from their father. In fact, 69 percent of the fathers of AFDC children recognized their children by helping the children and their mothers out, and by providing the children with kinship affiliations. These children's father's kin assumed an active role in their nurturing.

The importance of the kinship links a child acquires through his mother and father is demonstrated in fostering patterns. Table 4, derived from the AFDC survey, shows the residence of children temporarily fostered in households of kinsmen at a given time.

TABLE 4

Patterns of Child-Keeping, AFDC Data

	FREQUENCY	PERCENTAGE
Mother's kin	57	74
Father's kin	20	26
	77	100

Individual life histories reveal changes that have occurred in the residence of people in The Flats over the past fifty years. The data show the residence patterns of children fostered between 1925 and 1971. Table 5 shows residence patterns of children fostered in the households of kinsmen based on information derived from life histories of adults and children.

TABLE 5

Patterns of Child-Keeping, Residence Histories

	FREQUENCY	PERCENTAGE
Mother's kin	43	69
Father's kin	19	31
	62	100

The ratio of children kept in the homes of kinsmen related through a child's mother or father is approximately the same in Table 4 and Table 5. Although the majority of children in this study lived with their mother or her kin, based on the statistical study of AFDC histories, one-fourth of the fostered children lived with their father's kin. Based on life histories, one-third of all children fostered are living with their father's kin.

When mothers apply for AFDC benefits for their dependent children, they are required to list, in order of rank, whom they expect to raise each of their children if they die or are unable to maintain custody of the child. The responses of mothers in Table 6 reflect their "expectations" regarding which kinsmen would be willing and able to raise their child.

When asked by welfare workers who they would expect to raise their child in the event of their own death, mothers of 228 children named their own blood relatives; mothers of 76 children named the child's father's kin. The agreement between the expectations of adult females regarding child-keeping and the statistical patterns of child-keeping over the life cycle is striking.

TABLE 6

Child-Keeping Expectations, AFDC Data

	FREQUENCY	PERCENTAGE
Mother's kin	222	73
Father's kin	83	27
	305	100

The data obtained from AFDC case histories on the nurturing and fostering of children in The Flats, and from the life histories of people I knew well, suggest shared community expectations of rights and duties toward children. Both a child's mother's and father's socially recognized kinsmen are expected to assume parental rights and duties, and these expectations are borne out by actual events (Table 4 and Table 5). These predictable, stable child-keeping patterns provide a commanding contrast to the characterization of the black family life as "broken" and "disorganized."

TRANSACTIONS IN PARENTHOOD

When and why kin can become "parents" is a matter of folk rights and duties in relation to children. The content of rights and duties in relation to children differs cross-culturally; residents in The Flats find it difficult to spell out particular rights and duties in children. The elaboration of rights pertaining to children is best elicited from observed scenes.

Scenes in which rights in children are in conflict must be analyzed in terms of the social context in which they occur. The social context of situations includes at least the following considerations: the participants present, the specific life histories of the participants, the socially meaningful occurrences, which preceded the event, and the rules which come into play. The scenes described below reflect tension or conflict among kinsmen over rights in children. These scenes provide a basis for identifying parental behaviors which may be shared.

The first scene takes place on the front porch of a house which Georgia and her three children share with Georgia's middle-aged Aunt Ethel and Ethel's boyfriend. Just before the incident occurred, Georgia and Ethel had fought over the division of housework and the utility bills. Aunt Ethel was angered at Georgia's lack of respect and her unwillingness to support her with the AFDC benefits Georgia received for her children. Georgia was willing to pay the rent but insisted that Ethel's boyfriend pay the utilities and that Ethel take over more of the cooking and housework. Following the argument, Ethel's brother dropped by to visit. Ethel, her boyfriend, and her brother sat in the sunshine on the porch. Georgia and her children joined them. Georgia's daughter Alice was bothered by her first loose tooth. Alice continued whimpering on the porch as she had for most of the afternoon.

SCENE ONE

Aunt Ethel yanked Alice's arm, drawing Alice nearer to her on the porch. Trouble over Alice's loose tooth had gone far enough. Ethel decided to pull the tooth. Without nudging it to see how loose it really was, Ethel fixed her fingers on the tooth and pulled with all her strength. Alice screamed with fear, kicked, and tried to bite her aunt. Alice's mother, Georgia, sat nearby, her tense body and bulging eyes voicing silent resistance to her aunt's physical act. After some moments of the struggle passed, a friend who happened to be visiting said, "Maybe the tooth isn't ready, Ethel," and Ethel let the child go. Georgia's tensed face and body relaxed as her daughter sprang into her arms in tears. Georgia turned to her friend, her eyelids lowered, expressing relief that her friend's quick words had stopped Ethel's performance.

Georgia had lived in the same household with her mother's sister Ethel for most of her life. Ethel helped Georgia's grandmother raise her. After the grandmother's death, Ethel assumed responsibility for Georgia. Georgia's mother lived close by, but she had nine other children to raise on her own. Ethel has been married twice, but she never had any children. She refers to Georgia as her daughter even though she did not become head of the household in which Georgia was raised until Georgia was thirteen. In recent years Georgia has been much closer to her mother than to her aunt. Nevertheless, Ethel regards Georgia's children as her own grandchildren.

Ethel's assertive behavior with regard to Alice was not an isolated event. In Georgia's presence, Ethel frequently demonstrates the right she holds to love, discipline, and even terrify Georgia's children. Ethel feels intense love, obligation, and bitterness toward Georgia's children. Not so long ago Georgia left her children with Ethel and ran off with a serviceman. When Georgia returned six months later she complained that Ethel had neglected her children, their clothes, their hair, and had not fed them well.

In the context of the previous fight between Ethel and Georgia, Ethel's action is partly a performance. Ethel is demonstrating the rights which she shares and may be expected to assume in relation to Georgia's children; rights she assumed when she forcefully attempted to pull Alice's tooth. She was angered by Georgia's arrogance just minutes before. In response, Ethel strongly asserted and strengthened the rights she has in Georgia's children, rights which she simultaneously shares with Georgia.

Commenting on the event to me, Georgia said, "Whatever

happens to me, Ethel be the person to keep my kids. She already kept them once before. My mother, she ain't in no position to take them with all of her own, and I wouldn't have Aunt Flossie take them noway." But the episode disturbed Georgia. She didn't want to sit quietly and allow her child to be hurt, but she found herself powerless to act, considering her expectations that Ethel might be required to nurture her children.

The second scene takes place during a train ride to Chicago. It includes some of the same participants as those in the first scene. Kin to Ethel and Georgia rode the train together for a Fourth of July celebration with relatives. The group traveling together included Ethel's sisters Wilma and Ann, their children and grandchildren, and Georgia and her children—fourteen children in all.

SCENE TWO

The three sisters, Ethel, Wilma and Ann, sat toward the rear of the train, dressed fine for the occasion, ignoring the children's noise. Georgia sat across from them with her girl friend. A Coke bottle struck against the iron foot railing broke into pieces. Shrieks of laughter traveled from seat to seat where most of the small children—all cousins—were sitting together in the front of the train. Instantly Ethel walked forward to the front of the train by Wilma's young boy and began beating him harshly with her handbag. Then, showing she meant business, Ethel grabbed the boy next to the window who was laughing and gave him a few sharp slaps on the cheek. Wilma paid no attention to the cries of her two young boys. But when Ethel returned to her seat, Ann told her, "Don't you lay a hand on my granddaughter."

Throughout the trip Ethel shouted at, beat, and teased the children. Her sisters enjoyed the train ride and generally ignored the children. But Ethel's rights regarding each of her sister's children are not equivalent. From time to time, Ethel helped Wilma raise her children, including Georgia. Ethel has cared for or lived with Georgia's children for the past five years. Her rights in Wilma's and Georgia's children are recognized by both the mothers and the children. During the train ride, in the presence of her sisters and her niece, Ethel demonstrated her right to discipline the children of these kin. Likewise, the children observed the authority Ethel had over them.

On the other hand, Ethel's sister Ann had been married and was living fairly well. Ann was not an active participant in the domestic network of the sisters: she did not participate in the daily flow of exchanges among the sisters, and more often than not, Ann avoided exchanges of services which might obligate her to her sisters. Ann's daughters are self-supporting adults. It is quite unlikely that Ethel, Wilma, or Georgia would be expected or be required to raise Ann's granddaughters. In fact, Ann and her daughters consider themselves "better" than Ethel and Wilma. Usually Ann does not even allow her granddaughters to play with Wilma's children except for short periods of time. Rights over children come into conflict indicating who is excluded from parental rights in children. The third scene provides an example of who is not eligible to assume parental behavior patterns.

Vilda, Ann's daughter and Ethel's niece, had the opportunity to get a job she wanted. But she had to begin work immediately. Ann was working and Vilda had difficulty finding someone to care for her daughter Betty, who was four years old. She asked her cousin Georgia to take care of her daughter during the day and offered to pay her ten dollars a week.

SCENE THREE

Betty cried and put up a fuss at breakfast because she didn't want her mother to go to work, and she didn't want to stay at her Aunt Georgia's house. Betty said that Georgia beat her and yelled at her. Vilda and her mother, Ann, took the child to Georgia's house together that morning. They told Georgia that they didn't want her to yell or lay a hand on Betty.

This incident clearly communicated to Georgia that her cousin did not respect her and did not consider her an equal. Georgia made a big issue over this event to her friends and close kin. She said that Ann and Vilda were spoiling Betty and that "Betty was nothing but a brat." In turn, Georgia was unwilling to share rights in her children with Vilda and Ann. During the following summer, at a large family barbecue with many kin and friends present, Georgia made this clear.

SCENE FOUR

Georgia's daughter took a hot poker from the fire and ran after the younger children, threatening them. Ann quickly took the poker away from her niece and slapped her. Georgia jumped into the scene, grabbed her daughter from Ann and said, "You won't let me touch your granddaughter, so don't you tell my child what to do."

Although it is common for rights in children to be distributed among close female kin in The Flats, Scene Four shows that standards other than kin criteria are operative. Ann is not an active participant in the domestic network of her sisters; she and her husband are both employed and economically secure. Ann is the adult female kin least likely to be willing to accept responsibility for her nieces, nephews, and grandnieces and grandnephews.

Scenes One and Two are examples of circumstances in which a cluster of parental rights (the discipline of children, administering folk cures, and so forth) are shared by the biological mother along with eligible kin who are common members of her household. There are, however, circumstances in which clusters of rights and entailing behaviors are transferred from one individual to another. In these situations, mothers still retain the folk and legal right to acquire physical custody over their child if the right is disputed, the right to take their child as heir, and the rights of cognatic descent. But the major cluster of behavioral entailments of parenthood are shared or transferred to the woman currently raising the child.

Within the folk system of shared parental rights in children, time and intent play an important role. How long a child resides in a household apart from his mother may determine the extent to which the mother, in the eyes of the community, retains or transfers rights in the child to the responsible female. Likewise, whether the biological mother views the situation as a permanent or a temporary response to her personal problems is an important factor.

In Scene Five a young mother, Violet, married and moved to another state with her husband and her two youngest children by a previous union. She left her two older daughters with their grandmother (mother's mother), Bessie, because at the time the couple could not afford to take them along. Violet intended the situation to be temporary, but it lasted over seven months. Before Violet left the state she told Bessie not to let her children see their father. Violet feared that the father would try to acquire custody of the children by claiming that she had deserted them. After about seven months Violet learned through gossip that her children were spending a lot of time with their father and had been staying with him on weekends. She took the train back home as soon as she could in order to get her daughters and take them to her new home out of state.

SCENE FIVE

Violet was angered by her mother's decision to let her granddaughters stay with their father every weekend. She told her mother, "You wasn't s'posed to let him see them." Bessie said to Violet, "You ain't doing nothing for your children— the children are lucky their father and his kin take an interest in them."

Two issues complicate this situation. While Violet was living in The Flats with her children, she was willing to have her children's father buy their clothes and take them places. At least once a month the children would spend the weekend with their father at his sister's house. But when the father began "keeping house" with a new girl friend, Violet became very jealous and told her friends, "The girl wants to take my babies from me."

The issue of paternity is a further complication in this scene. The father considered himself father only to Violet's oldest child. Violet told her second-born child that she and the oldest child had the same daddy. The father's kin showed much more concern and responsibility toward the oldest child and teased Violet, saying, "Soon, girl, you going to push all your children off on him." When Violet was in town she demanded that this man treat her two oldest children as his own. One time the second child became very emotionally upset when the father said to her, "I ain't your daddy." Violet was afraid that in her absence he would say it again, or hurt the child. Although Violet's mother was aware of both of these issues, she decided that while she was responsible for her grandchildren, she would decide what was best for them. Bessie exercised the rights she acquired in her grandchildren when Violet left town and left her children.

The conflict between Violet and Bessie over this issue was so great that Violet returned to town to regain physical custody of her children. Late one winter evening, she rode the Greyhound bus into The Flats with winter coats for her two daughters. She took a cab to her mother's home, woke her daughters, put on their coats, and took the same cab back to the bus station. Within two hours Violet and her daughters were on their way out of town. The father had no knowledge of what had happened until several days later. He made no attempt to contact Violet.

Violet did not have enough money with her to buy tickets to travel out of the state. In fact, she only had enough money to buy one-way tickets to Chicago. She and her daughters took the bus to Chicago and she called one of her closest girl friends, Samantha, to pick them up at the bus station. Violet and her daughters stayed with Samantha and her three children for nearly a month.

Violet and Samantha considered themselves kin. They lived down the street from one another while they were growing up, attended the same schools, and dated boys who were close cousins or best friends. Five years ago, just after Samantha gave birth to her second child, she became very ill. Violet insisted upon "taking" Samantha's year-old son in order to help her.

Scene Six was told to me by Violet three years after the event.

SCENE SIX

That day I went over to visit Samantha, I don't know how the good Lord tell me, since I hadn't been seeing her for some time. The last old man she had didn't like me, so I stayed away. He sure was no good. Left her right before the baby come.

I went over to her place. She had a small, dark little room with a kitchen for herself and those two babies. The place look bad and smell bad. I knew she was hurting. I took one look around and said to her, "Samantha, I'm going to take your boy." I hunted up some diapers and left the house with her year-old son. She didn't come by my place for over a month, but her younger sister brought me a message that Samantha was feeling better. A week or two later she came by to visit. Her boy hardly knew her. She came by more often, but she still seemed pretty low. I told her one day, "Samantha, I don't have any sons, just daughters, so why don't you just give me this boy." She said that if he didn't favor his father so much she'd let me keep him, but she was still crazy over that man. Her boy stayed with me three or four months, then she came and got him. Soon afterwards she moved to Chicago with her two kids and her new old man.

When friends in The Flats have good social dealings with one another they often call each other by kin terms and conduct their social relations as if they were kinsmen. Close kin form alliances with one another to cope with daily needs. Close friends assume the same style of dealing with one another. Samantha and Violet shared an exchange of goods and services over the years and lived up to one another's expectations. They obligated, tested, and trusted one another.

The exchange of children, and short-term fosterage, are common among female friends. Child-care arrangements among friends imply both rights and duties. Close friends frequently discipline each other's children verbally and physically in front of each other. In normal times, and in times of stress, close friends have the right to "ask" for one another's children. A woman visiting a friend and her children may say, "Let me keep your girl this week. She will have a fine time with me and my girls. She won't want to come back home to her mama." This kind of request among kin and friends is very difficult to refuse.

Temporary child-care services are also a means of obligating kin or friends for future needs. Women may ask to "keep" the child of a friend for no apparent reason. But they are, in fact, building up an investment for their future needs. From this perspective it is clear that child-keeping in The Flats is both an expression of shared kin obligations toward children and an important feature of the distribution and exchange of the limited resources available to poor people in The Flats.

The scenes in which conflicts arise between kin over rights in children provide a basis for pinpointing the patterns of rights and duties in relation to children in The Flats.[3] From the viewpoint of the white middle class the kinship term "mother" is an idealized combination of behavioral roles expected to be assumed by a single person (Keesing 1969). In striking contrast, the scenes just described are illustrations of a sharing among close kinsmen of obligations toward children.

Close female kinsmen in The Flats do not expect a single person, the natural mother, to carry out by herself all of the behavior patterns which "motherhood" entails. When transactions between females over the residence, care and discipline of children run smoothly, it is difficult to clarify the patterns of rights and duties to which kin and non-kin are entitled. But scenes in which these rights and duties come into conflict show which behaviors may be shared.

Keesing (1970b, p. 432) suggests that "where the division of behaviors usually performed by a single actor among two or more actors follows lines of cleavage established by and standardized in the culture, then we are dealing with separate 'social identities.' " Goodenough (1965, p. 3) has defined social identity as "an aspect of self that makes a difference in how one's rights and duties distribute with respect to specific others." A kin term such as "mother" entails a cluster of social identities which we will define as distinguishable social positions. A set of appropriate behavior patterns apply to each social position; and more than one person can occupy the same social position at the same time (Keesing 1969; 1970b). For example, if two or more women customarily assume behavioral roles toward individual children which could be performed by a single person, then these women occupy a social position which has behavioral entailments with respect to those children.

Scenes from the preceding section illustrate patterns of rights and duties toward children in The Flats and furnish examples of social positions which kinsmen occupy with respect to one another's children. As stated earlier, it is impossible to fully elaborate the rights and duties in children within a culture. But from scenes in which these rights come into conflict, some of the following more apparent social positions stand out (Keesing 1970b): provider, discipliner, trainer, curer, and groomer.

These social positions represent the composite of typical parental behaviors which may be shared primarily among a child's close female kinsmen. They are categories of behavior which have predictable, non-legal rights and obligations.

Economic providers are expected to share in providing subsistence and scarce goods, daily meals, food stamps, a bed, a blanket, clothes and shoes. Discipliners (primarily women) are allowed to participate in the control of children. At their own discretion they may beat—usually with a green branch stripped of leaves—threaten, terrify, blame, or scare children for unacceptable social behavior. Trainers not only discipline but teach moral values and respect for adults. They instruct by example, teaching children the consequences of their acts. A girl is taught to sit like a lady—even a two-year-old would be slapped for sitting with her legs apart, or a three-year-old boy might be chastised for hugging or touching a two-year-old girl. The consequences are taught by trainers by harsh, clear example. One afternoon Ruby's four-year-old daughter and my son Kevin were bored from being kept indoors on a cold winter day. The four-year-old grabbed a book of matches from the kitchen and was lighting them one by one, and both children were blowing them out with great joy. Ruby and I were talking in the dining room. She saw what was happening, rushed over, and held a burning match to her daughter's arm, slightly blistering the skin. An adult may, for example, yell at a noisy child, "I'll tear your eyes!", or "I'm going to beat your black ass until it's red as burning coals!" The older children often repeat such phrases in their discipline of the younger children. Curers provide folk remedies for physical ailments. They have the right to attempt to heal rashes with a little lye or detergent in the bath water, remove warts, pull teeth, and cure stomach ailments of children with "persnickety"—a pungent brew made from tobacco and added to the baby's milk. A groomer has the obligation to care for the children, wash clothing, and check the children's bodies for rashes and diseases. In addition to eligible adults, older females are also expected to groom younger children.

Adult females who share parental rights in children are recruited from participants in the personal domestic networks of the child's mother. This includes cognatic kin to the mother, the child, and close friends. Social roles such as that of provider were often shared; thus, responsibilities were seen to have composite elements and the various parts could be assumed by more than one individual. For example, a woman who lived next door to Ruby left her three children with her sister. The sister fed and clothed the children, took them to the doctor, and made all the other necessary decisions with respect to their lives. But, the rights that eligible kinsmen or close friends share in one another's children are not equal. Other factors such as economics and interpersonal relationships within domestic networks come into play. In white middle-class families, on the other hand, few persons, not even kin, would be authorized or would feel free to participate in health care or disciplinary behavior with regard to children without specific permission or transfer (care of a child in case of a parent's illness), or except in the case of an emergency.

A detailed look at scenes from preceding sections provides important clues about eligibility.

Scene One. What factors underlie the mutual expectations that Ethel and Georgia share concerning Ethel's rights in Georgia's children?

1. Ethel raised Georgia and assumes grandparental rights in Georgia's children.
2. Ethel assumed full responsibility for Georgia's children when Georgia abandoned them and left town temporarily with a serviceman.
3. The behavior patterns which Ethel assumes with respect to Georgia's children are appropriate, independent of whether or not they are co-resident.
4. In the presence of others Ethel frequently exhibits the rights she shares in Georgia's children and Georgia acknowledges these rights.

It appears that Ethel is demonstrating the rights which she shares and may be expected to assume in Georgia's children. Georgia's own words reinforce this interpretation; "Whatever happens to me, Ethel be the person to keep my kids."

Scenes two, three, four, and six illustrate that standards other than kin criteria effectively exclude individuals from assuming parental rights in children. Close friends who are active participants in domestic networks may be expected to "keep" children. On the other hand, relatives who are not participants in the domestic networks of kinsmen are not eligible to assume parental roles:

1. Ann was not a participant in the domestic network of her sisters.
2. Ann is excluded from parental rights in her sister's and niece's children.
3. Ann's sisters do not have parental rights in Ann's children or grandchildren.

These situations show that even siblings' rights regarding sister's children are not equivalent.

Kin and friends in domestic networks establish mutual ties of obligation as they bestow rights and responsibilities upon one another. As these responsibilities are met with satisfaction, the depth of the involvement between kinsmen and between friends increases. Simultaneously, females acquire reciprocal obligations toward one another's children and rights in them. As responsibilities toward specific children are amplified, females are ultimately allowed to occupy parental roles toward children which are recognized by both adults and children. When women consciously perform duties as provider, discipliner, trainer, curer, and groomer, then they have accepted the reality that they may be required to nurture these children. These are the women who are next in line to nurture and assume custody of the children to whom their obligations apply.

Our concern up to now has not been with motherhood itself, but with the criteria by which rights and duties in children distribute socially and may be delegated to other kinsmen. At this point it is necessary to take a close look at Goodenough's definition of jural motherhood:

> If we try to define jural motherhood by the kinds of rights and duties comprising it, we are in trouble, as the societies we have already considered reveal. For the ways in which rights in children distribute socially and the very content of the rights themselves vary considerably cross-culturally. We are dealing with a jural role, then, but can identify it cross-culturally not by its content but by some constant among the criteria by which people are entitled to the role (1970, p. 24).
> With the foregoing in mind, we may say that jural motherhood consists of the rights and duties a woman has claim to in relation to a child by virtue of her having borne it, provided she is eligible to bear it and provided no other disqualifying circumstances attend its birth (1970, p. 25).

Potential nurturers of children share or transfer non-jural rights in children in the process of child-keeping. Individuals do not acquire rights of motherhood in the temporary exchange of children. But some child-keeping situations which are intended to be temporary become permanent. And child-keeping can ultimately involve the transfer of rights in children.

There is no specific time period after which child-keeping becomes a permanent transfer of rights in the eyes of the community. The intentions which the jural mother makes public, the frequency of her visits, the extent to which she continues to provide for the child, and the extent to which she continues to occupy all of the social positions of parenthood are all factors in sanctions over rights in children.

Some mothers whose children are being kept by kin or friends eventually stop visiting and providing goods and services for their children. In such cases, the child-keeper may ultimately become the parent in the eyes of the community. Later attempts by the biological mother to regain custody of her child may be met with disapproval, threats, and gossip within the domestic group.

In the eyes of the community, individuals who acquire rights in children have the right to make decisions over the subsequent transfer of custody of the child. In one situation a great-grandfather "kept" his great-granddaughter for eight years. During this time the mother showed little concern for her daughter, and the great-grandfather came to be considered the child's parent. When the grandfather decided that he was too old to care for the child, the mother wanted the child back. But he decided to give custody to another relative whom he considered more responsible. This decision was supported by their kinsmen. As the daughter herself said, "I was staying with my great-grandfather for the first five years of my life, but he just got too old to care for me. My mother was living in The Flats at the time, but my 'daddy' asked my mother's brother and his wife to take me 'cause he really trusted them with me."

Folk sanctions concerning the transfer of rights in children are often in conflict with the publicly sanctioned laws of the state. The courts are more likely to award custody of a child to its biological mother rather than to other kinsmen. Individuals in The Flats operate within the folk and legal system. Mothers have successfully taken close kinsmen (their own mother or aunt, for example) to court in order to regain custody of their natural children. But such acts are strongly discouraged by people who regard children as a mutual responsibility of the kin group. Children born to the poor in The Flats are highly valued, and rights in these children belong to the networks of cooperating kinsmen.[4] Shared parental responsibilities are not only an obligation of kinship, they constitute a highly cherished right. Attempts of outside social agencies, the courts, or the police to control the residence, guardianship, or behavior of children are thwarted by the domestic group. Such efforts are interpreted in The Flats as attempts on the part of the larger society to control and manipulate their children.

6

DOMESTIC NETWORKS

"Those You Count On"

In The Flats the responsibility for providing food, care, clothing, and shelter and for socializing children within domestic networks may be spread over several households. Which household a given individual belongs to is not a particularly meaningful question, as we have seen that daily domestic organization depends on several things: where people sleep, where they eat, and where they offer their time and money. Although those who eat together and contribute toward the rent are generally considered by Flat's residents to form minimal domestic units, household changes rarely affect the exchanges and daily dependencies of those who take part in common activity.

The residence patterns and cooperative organization of people linked in domestic networks demonstrate the stability and collective power of family life in The Flats. Michael Lee grew up in The Flats and now has a job in Chicago. On a visit to The Flats, Michael described the residence and domestic organization of his kin. "Most of my kin in The Flats lived right here on Cricket Street, numbers sixteen, eighteen, and twenty-two, in these three apartment buildings joined together. My mama decided it would be best for me and my three brothers and sister to be on Cricket Street too. My daddy's mother had a small apartment in this building, her sister had one in the basement, and another brother and his family took a larger apartment upstairs. My uncle was really good to us. He got us things we wanted and he controlled us. All the women kept the younger kids together during the day. They cooked together too. It was good living."

Yvonne Diamond, a forty-year-old Chicago woman, moved to The Flats from Chicago with her four children. Soon afterwards they were evicted. "The landlord said he was going to build a parking lot there, but he never did. The old place is still standing and has folks in it today. My husband's mother and father took me and the kids in and watched over them while I had my baby. We stayed on after my husband's mother died, and my husband joined us when he got a job in The Flats."

When families or individuals in The Flats are evicted, other kinsmen usually take them in. Households in The Flats expand or contract with the loss of a job, a death in the family, the beginning or end of a sexual partnership, or the end of a friendship. Welfare workers, researchers, and landlords have long known that the poor must move frequently. What is much less understood is the relationship between residence and domestic organization in the black community.

The spectrum of economic and legal pressures that act upon ghetto residents, requiring them to move—unemployment, welfare requirements, housing shortages, high rents, eviction— are clear-cut examples of external pressures affecting the daily lives of the poor. Flats' residents are evicted from their dwellings by landlords who want to raise rents, tear the building down, or rid themselves of tenants who complain about rats, roaches, and the plumbing. Houses get condemned by the city on landlords' requests so that they can force tenants to move. After an eviction, a landlord can rent to a family in such great need of housing that they will not complain for a while.

Poor housing conditions and unenforced housing standards coupled with overcrowding, unemployment, and poverty produce hazardous living conditions and residence changes. "Our whole family had to move when the gas lines sprung a leak in

our apartment and my son set the place on fire by accident,"
Sam Summer told me. "The place belonged to my sister-in-
law's grandfather. We had been living there with my mother,
my brother's eight children, and our eight children. My father
lived in the basement apartment 'cause he and my mother were
separated. After the fire burned the whole place down, we all
moved to two places down the street near my cousin's house."

When people are unable to pay their rent because they have
been temporarily "cut off aid," because the welfare office is
suspicious of their eligibility, because they gave their rent money
to a kinsman to help him through a crisis or illness, or because they were laid off from their job, they receive eviction
notices almost immediately. Lydia Watson describes a chain
of events starting with the welfare office stopping her sister's
welfare checks, leading to an eviction, co-residence, overcrowding, and eventually murder. Lydia sadly related the story to me.
"My oldest sister was cut off aid the day her husband got out
of jail. She and her husband and their three children were
evicted from their apartment and they came to live with us. We
were in crowded conditions already. I had my son, my other
sister was there with her two kids, and my mother was about
going crazy. My mother put my sister's husband out 'cause she
found out he was a dope addict. He came back one night soon
after that and murdered my sister. After my sister's death my
mother couldn't face living in Chicago any longer. One of my
other sisters who had been adopted and raised by my mother's
paternal grandmother visited us and persuaded us to move to
The Flats, where she was staying. All of us moved there—my
mother, my two sisters and their children, my two baby sisters,
and my dead sister's children. My sister who had been staying
in The Flats found us a house across the street from her own."

Overcrowded dwellings and the impossibility of finding
adequate housing in The Flats have many long-term consequences regarding where and with whom children live.

Terence Platt described where and with whom his kin lived when he was a child. "My brother stayed with my aunt, my mother's sister, and her husband until he was ten, 'cause he was the oldest in our family and we didn't have enough room —but he stayed with us most every weekend. Finally my aunt moved into the house behind ours with her husband, her brother, and my brother; my sisters and brothers and I lived up front with my mother and her old man."

KIN-STRUCTURED LOCAL NETWORKS

The material and cultural support needed to absorb, sustain, and socialize community members in The Flats is provided by networks of cooperating kinsmen. Local coalitions formed from these networks of kin and friends are mobilized within domestic networks; domestic organization is diffused over many kin-based households which themselves have elastic boundaries.

People in The Flats are immersed in a domestic web of a large number of kin and friends whom they can count on. From a social viewpoint, relationships within the community are "organized on the model of kin relationships" (Goodenough 1970, p. 49). Kin-constructs such as the perception of parenthood, the culturally determined criteria which affect the shape of personal kindreds, and the idiom of kinship, prescribe kin who can be recruited into domestic networks.

There are similarities in function between domestic networks and domestic groups which Fortes (1962, p. 2) characterizes as "workshops of social reproduction." Both domains include three generations of members linked collaterally or otherwise. Kinship, jural and affectional bonds, and economic factors affect the composition of both domains and residential alignments within them. There are two striking differences between domestic networks and domestic groups. Domestic networks are not visible groups, because they do not have an obvious nucleus or defined boundary. But since a primary focus of domestic networks is child-care arrangements, the cooperation of a cluster of adult females is apparent. Participants in domestic networks are recruited from personal kindreds and friendships, but the personnel changes with fluctuating economic needs, changing life styles, and vacillating personal relationships.

In some loosely and complexly structured cognatic systems, kin-structured local networks (not groups) emerge. Localized coalitions of persons drawn from personal kindreds can be organized as networks of kinsmen. Goodenough (1970, p. 49) correctly points out that anthropologists frequently describe "localized kin groups," but rarely describe kin-structured local groups (Goodenough 1962; Helm 1965). The localized, kin-based, cooperative coalitions of people described in this chapter are organized as kin-structured domestic networks. For brevity, I refer to them as domestic networks.[1]

RESIDENCE AND DOMESTIC ORGANIZATION

The connection between households and domestic life can be illustrated by examples taken from cooperating kinsmen and friends mobilized within domestic networks in The Flats. Domestic networks are, of course, not centered around one individual, but for simplicity the domestic network in the following example is named for the key participants in the network, Magnolia and Calvin Waters. The description is confined to four months between April and July 1969. Even within this short time span, individuals moved and joined other households within the domestic network.

THE DOMESTIC NETWORK OF MAGNOLIA AND CALVIN WATERS

Magnolia Waters is forty-one years old and has eleven children. At sixteen she moved from the South with her parents, four sisters (Augusta, Carrie, Lydia, and Olive), and two brothers (Pennington and Oscar). Soon after this she gave birth to her oldest daughter, Ruby. At twenty-three Ruby Banks had two daughters and a son, each by a different father.

When Magnolia was twenty-five she met Calvin, who was forty-seven years old. They lived together and had six children. Calvin is now sixty-three years old; Calvin and Magnolia plan to marry soon so that Magnolia will receive Calvin's insurance benefits. Calvin has two other daughters, who are thirty-eight and forty, by an early marriage in Mississippi. Calvin still has close ties with his daughters and their mother who all live near one another with their families in Chicago.

Magnolia's oldest sister, Augusta, is childless and has not been married. Augusta has maintained long-term "housekeeping" partnerships with four different men over the past twenty years, and each of them has helped her raise her sisters' children. These men have maintained close, affectional ties with the family over the years. Magnolia's youngest sister, Carrie, married Lazar, twenty-five years her senior, when she was just fifteen. They stayed together for about five years. After they separated Carrie married Kermit, separated from him, and became an alcoholic. She lives with different men from time to time, but in between men, or when things are at loose ends, she stays with Lazar, who has become a participating member of the family. Lazar usually resides near Augusta and Augusta's "old man," and Augusta generally prepares Lazar's meals. Ever since Carrie became ill, Augusta has been raising Carrie's son.

Magnolia's sister Lydia had two daughters, Lottie and Georgia, by two different fathers, before she married Mike and gave birth to his son. After Lydia married Mike, she no longer received AFDC benefits for her children. Lydia and Mike acquired steady jobs, bought a house and furniture, and were doing very well. For at least ten years they purposely removed themselves from the network of kin cooperation, preventing their kin from draining their resources. They refused to participate in the network of exchanges which Lydia had formerly depended upon; whenever possible they refused to trade clothes or lend money, or if they gave something, they did not ask for anything in return. During this period they were not participants in the domestic network. About a year ago Lydia and Mike separated over accusations and gossip that each of them had established another sexual relationship. During the five-month-period when the marriage was ending, Lydia began giving some of her nice clothes away to her sisters and nieces. She gave a couch to her brother and a TV to a niece. Anticipating her coming needs, Lydia attempted to reobligate her kin by carrying out the pattern which had been a part of her daily life before her marriage. After Lydia separated from her husband, her two younger children once again received AFDC. Lydia's oldest daughter, Lottie, is over eighteen and too old to receive AFDC, but Lottie has a three-year-old daughter who has received AFDC benefits since birth.

Eloise has been Magnolia's closest friend for many years. Eloise is Magnolia's first son's father's sister. This son moved into his father's household by his own choice when he was about twelve years old. Magnolia and Eloise have maintained a close, sisterly friendship. Eloise lives with her husband, her four children, and the infant son of her oldest daughter, who is seventeen. Eloise's husband's brother's daughter, Lily, who is twenty, and her young daughter recently joined the household. Eloise's husband's youngest brother is the father of her sister's child. When the child was an infant, that sister stayed with Eloise and her husband.

Billy Jones lives in the basement in the same apartment house as Augusta, Magnolia's sister. A temperamental woman with three sons, Billy has become Augusta's closest friend. Billy once ran a brothel in The Flats, but she has worked as a cook, has written songs, and has attended college from time to time. Augusta keeps Billy's sons whenever Billy leaves town, has periods of depression, or beats the children too severely.

Another active participant in the network is Willa Mae. Willa Mae's younger brother, James, is Ruby's daughter's father. Even though James does not visit the child and has not assumed any parental duties toward the child, Willa Mae and Ruby, who are the same age, help each other out with their young children.

Calvin's closest friend, Cecil, died several years ago. Cecil was Violet's husband. Violet, Cecil, and Calvin came from the same town in Mississippi and their families have been very close. Calvin boarded with Violet's family for five years or so before he met Magnolia. Violet is now seventy years old. She lives with her daughter, Odessa, who is thirty-seven, her two sons, Josh, who is thirty-five and John, who is forty, and Odessa's three sons and daughter. Odessa's husband was killed in a fight several years ago and ever since then she and her family have shared a household with Violet and her two grown sons. Violet's sons Josh and John are good friends with Magnolia, Ruby, and Augusta and visit them frequently. About five years ago John brought one of his daughters to live with his mother and sister because his family thought that the mother was not taking proper care of the child; the mother had several other children and did not object. The girl is now ten years old and is an accepted member of the family and the network.

Chart C shows the spatial relations of the households in Magnolia and Calvin's domestic network in April 1969. The houses are scattered within The Flats, but none of them is more than three miles apart. Cab fare, up to two dollars per trip, is spent practically every day, and sometimes twice a day, as individuals visit, trade, and exchange services. Chart D shows how individuals are brought into the domestic network.

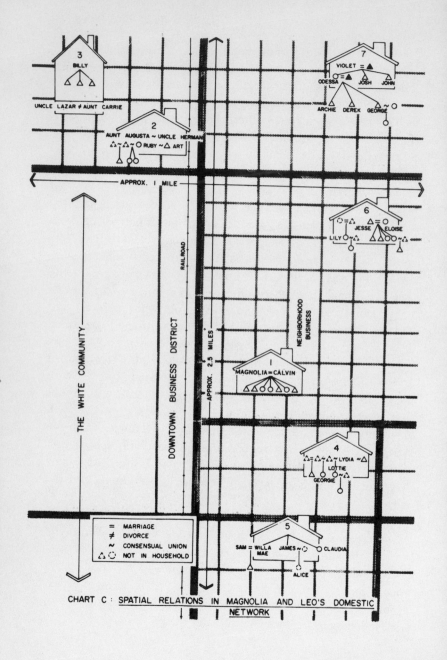

CHART C: SPATIAL RELATIONS IN MAGNOLIA AND LEO'S DOMESTIC
NETWORK

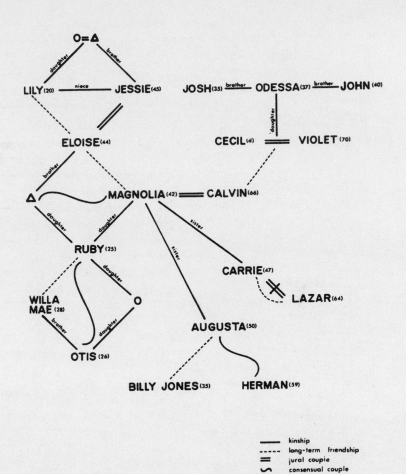

CHART D : KIN-STRUCTURED DOMESTIC NETWORK

O=△

LILY (20) — niece — JESSIE (45)   JOSH (35) — brother — ODESSA (37) — brother — JOHN (40)
daughter   brother

ELOISE (44)   CECIL (d) ═══ VIOLET (70)

△   MAGNOLIA (42) ═══ CALVIN (66)
brother

daughter   daughter   sister   CARRIE (47)

RUBY (25)   sister   LAZAR (64)

daughter   AUGUSTA (50)

WILLA MAE (28)   O

brother   daughter

OTIS (26)   BILLY JONES (35)   HERMAN (59)

————— kinship
- - - - - long-term friendship
═══ jural couple
∿ consensual couple
O △ not in network

The following outline shows residential changes which occurred in several of the households within the network between April and June 1969.

APRIL 1969

Household   *Domestic Arrangement*

1 Magnolia (38) and Calvin (60) live in a common-law relationship with their eight children (ages 4 to 18).

2 Magnolia's sister Augusta and Augusta's "old man," Herman, share a two-bedroom house with Magnolia's daughter Ruby (22) and Ruby's three children. Augusta and Herman have one bedroom, the three children sleep in the second bedroom, and Ruby sleeps downstairs in the living room. Ruby's boyfriend, Art, stays with Ruby many evenings.

3 Augusta's girl friend Billy and Billy's three sons live on the first floor of the house. Lazar, Magnolia's and Augusta's ex-brother-in-law, lives in the basement alone, or from time to time, with his ex-wife Carrie. Lazar eats the evening meal, which Augusta prepares for him, at household #2.

4 Magnolia's sister Lydia, Lydia's "old man," Lydia's two daughters, Georgia and Lottie, Lydia's son, and Lottie's three-year-old daughter live in Lydia's house.

5 Willa Mae (26), her husband, her son, her sister Claudia (32), and her brother James (father of Ruby's daughter) share a household.

6 Eloise (37), her husband Jessie, their four children, their oldest daughter's (17) son, and Jessie's brother's daughter Lily (20), and Lily's baby all live together.

7 Violet (70), her two sons, Josh (35) and John (40), her daughter Odessa (37), and Odessa's three sons and one daughter live together. Five years ago John's daughter (10) joined the household.

JUNE 1969

Household   *Domestic Arrangement*

1 Household composition unchanged.

2 Augusta and Herman moved out after quarreling with Ruby over housekeeping and cooking duties. They joined household #3. Ruby

and Art remained in household #2 and began housekeeping with Ruby's children.

3 *Billy and her three sons remained on the first floor and Lazar remained in the basement. Augusta and Herman rented a small, one-room apartment upstairs.*

4 *Lottie and her daughter moved out of Lydia's house to a large apartment down the street, which they shared with Lottie's girl friend and the friend's daughter. Georgia moved into her boyfriend's apartment. Lydia and her son (17) remained in the house with Lydia's "old man."*

5 *James began housekeeping with a new girl friend who lived with her sister, but he kept most of his clothes at home. His brother moved into his room after returning from the service. Willa Mae, her husband, and son remained in the house.*

6 *Household composition unchanged.*

7 *Odessa's son Raymond is the father of Clover's baby. Clover and the baby joined the household which includes Violet, her two sons, her daughter, Odessa, and Odessa's three sons and one daughter and John's daughter.*

Typical residential alignments in The Flats are those between adult mothers and sisters, mothers and adult sons and daughters, close adult female relatives, and friends defined as kin within the idiom of kinship. Domestic organization is diffused over these kin-based households.

Residence patterns among the poor in The Flats must be considered in the context of domestic organization. The connection between residence and domestic organization is apparent in examples of a series of domestic and child-care arrangements within Magnolia and Calvin's network a few years ago. Consider the following four kin-based residences among Magnolia and Calvin's kin in 1966.

Household   *Domestic Arrangement*

1 *Magnolia, Calvin, and seven young children.*

2 *Magnolia's mother, Magnolia's brother, Magnolia's sister and her*

sister's husband, Magnolia's oldest daughter, Ruby, and Ruby's first child.

3 *Magnolia's oldest sister, Augusta, Augusta's "old man," Augusta's sister's (Carrie) son, and Magnolia's twelve-year-old son.*

4 *Magnolia's oldest son, his father, and the father's "old lady."*

Household composition *per se* reveals little about domestic organization even when cooperation between close adult females is assumed. Three of these households (1, 2, 3) were located on one city block. Magnolia's mother rented a rear house behind Magnolia's house, and Magnolia's sister Augusta lived in an apartment down the street. As we have seen, they lived and shared each other's lives. Magnolia, Ruby, and Augusta usually pooled the food stamps they received from the welfare office. The women shopped together and everyone shared the evening meal with their men and children at Magnolia's mother's house or at Magnolia's. The children did not always have a bed of their own or a bed which they were expected to share with another child. They fell asleep and slept through the night wherever the late evening visiting patterns of the adult females took them.

The kinship links which most often are the basis of new or expanded households are those links children have with close adult females such as the child's mother, mother's mother, mother's sister, mother's brother's wife, father's mother, father's sister, and father's brother's wife.

Here are some examples of the flexibility of the Blacks' adaptation to daily, social, and economic problems (Stack 1970, p. 309).

Relational Link	Domestic Arrangement
Mother	*Viola's brother married his first wife when he was sixteen. When she left him she kept their daughter.*
Mother's mother	*Viola's sister Martha was never able to care for her children because of her nerves and high blood.*

	In between husbands, her mother kept her two oldest children, and after Martha's death, her mother kept all three of the children.
Mother's brother	*A year after Martha's death, Martha's brother took Martha's oldest daughter, helping his mother out since this left her with only two children to care for.*
Mother's mother	*Viola's daughter (20) was living at home and gave birth to a son. The daughter and her son remained in the Jackson household until the daughter married and set up a separate household with her husband, leaving her son to be raised by her mother.*
Mother's sister	*Martha moved to Chicago into her sister's household. The household consisted of the two sisters and four of their children.*
Father's mother	*Viola's sister Ethel had four daughters and one son. When Ethel had a nervous breakdown, her husband took the three daughters and his son to live with his mother in Arkansas. After his wife's death, the husband took the oldest daughter, to join her siblings in his mother's home in Arkansas.*
Father's mother	*When Viola's younger sister, Christine, left her husband in order to harvest fruit in Wisconsin, Christine left her two daughters with her husband's mother in Arkansas.*
Father's sister	*When Viola's brother's wife died, he decided to raise his two sons himself. He kept the two boys and never remarried although he had several girl friends and a child with one. His residence has always been near Viola's and she fed and cared for his sons.*

The basis of these cooperative units is mutual aid among siblings of both sexes, the domestic cooperation of close adult females, and the exchange of goods and services between male and female kin (Stack 1970). R. T. Smith (1970, p. 66) has referred to this pattern and observes that even when lower-class Blacks live in a nuclear family group, what is "most striking is the extent to which lower-class persons continue to be involved with other kin." Nancie Gonzalez (1970, p. 232) suggests that "the fact that individuals have simultaneous loyalties to more than one such grouping may be important in understanding the social structure as a whole."

These co-residential socializing units do indeed show the important role of the black female. But the cooperation between male and female siblings who share the same household or live near one another has been understimated by those who have considered the female-headed household and the grandmother-headed household (especially the mother's mother) as the most significant domestic units among the urban black poor.

The close cooperation of adults arises from the residential patterns typical of young adults. Due to poverty, young females with or without children do not perceive any choice but to remain living at home with their mother or other adult female relatives. Even if young women are collecting AFDC, they say that their resources go further when they share goods and services. Likewise, jobless males, or those working at part-time or seasonal jobs, often remain living at home with their mother or, if she is dead, with their sisters and brothers. This pattern continues long after men have become fathers and have established a series of sexual partnerships with women, who are living with their own kin, friends, or alone with their children. A result of this pattern is the striking fact that households almost always have men around: male relatives, by birth or marriage, and boyfriends. These men are often intermittent members of the households, boarders, or friends who come and go; men who usually eat, and sometimes sleep, in the households. Children have constant and close contact with these men, and especially in the case of male relatives, these relationships last over the years.

The most predictable residential pattern in The Flats is that men and women reside in one of the households of their natal kin, or in the households of those who raised them, long into their adult years. Even when persons temporarily move out of the household of their mother or of a close relative, they have the option to return to the residences of their kin if they have to.

GENEROSITY AND POVERTY

The combination of arbitrary and repressive economic forces and social behavior, modified by successive generations of poverty, make it almost impossible for people to break out of poverty. There is no way for those families poor enough to receive welfare to acquire any surplus cash which can be saved for emergencies or for acquiring adequate appliances or a home or a car. In contrast to the middle class, who are pressured to spend and save, the poor are not even permitted to establish an equity.

The following examples from Magnolia and Calvin Waters' life illustrates the ways in which the poor are prohibited from acquiring any surplus which might enable them to change their economic condition or life style.

In 1971 Magnolia's uncle died in Mississippi and left an unexpected inheritance of $1,500 to Magnolia and Calvin Waters. The cash came from a small run-down farm which Magnolia's uncle sold shortly before he died. It was the first time in their lives that Magnolia or Calvin ever had a cash reserve. Their first hope was to buy a home and use the money as a down payment.

Calvin had retired from his job as a seasonal laborer the year before and the family was on welfare. AFDC alloted the family $100 per month for rent. The housing that the family had been able to obtain over the years for their nine children at $100 or less was always small, roach infested, with poor plumbing and heating. The family was frequently evicted. Landlords complained about the noise and often observed an average of ten to fifteen children playing in the household. Magnolia and Calvin never even anticipated that they would be able to buy a home.

Three days after they received the check, news of its arrival spread throughout their domestic network. One niece borrowed $25 from Magnolia so that her phone would not be turned off. Within a week the welfare office knew about the money. Magnolia's children were immediately cut off welfare, including medical coverage and food stamps. Magnolia was told that she would not receive a welfare grant for her children until the money was used up, and she was given a minimum of four months in which to spend the money. The first surplus the family ever acquired was effectively taken from them.

During the weeks following the arrival of the money, Magnolia and Calvin's obligations to the needs of kin remained the same, but their ability to meet these needs had temporarily increased. When another uncle became very ill in the South, Magnolia and her older sister, Augusta, were called to sit by his side. Magnolia bought round-trip train tickets for both of them and for her three youngest children. When the uncle died, Magnolia bought round-trip train tickets so that she and Augusta could attend the funeral. Soon after his death, Augusta's first "old man" died in The Flats and he had no kin to pay for the burial. Augusta asked Magnolia to help pay for digging the grave. Magnolia was unable to refuse. Another sister's rent was two months overdue and Magnolia feared that she would get evicted. This sister was seriously ill and had no source of income. Magnolia paid her rent.

Winter was cold and Magnolia's children and grandchildren began staying home from school because they did not have warm winter coats and adequate shoes or boots. Magnolia and Calvin decided to buy coats, hats, and shoes for all of the children (at least fifteen). Magnolia also bought a winter coat for herself and Calvin bought himself a pair of sturdy shoes.

Within a month and a half, all of the money was gone. The money was channeled into the hands of the same individuals who ordinarily participate in daily domestic exchanges, but the premiums were temporarily higher. All of the money was quickly spent for necessary, compelling reasons.

Thus random fluctuations in the meager flow of available cash and goods tend to be of considerable importance to the poor. A late welfare check, sudden sickness, robbery, and other unexpected losses cannot be overcome with a cash reserve like more well-to-do families hold for emergencies. Increases in cash are either taken quickly from the poor by the welfare agencies or dissipated through the kin network.

Those living in poverty have little or no chance to escape from the economic situation into which they were born. Nor do they have the power to control the expansion or contraction of welfare benefits (Piven and Cloward 1971) or of employment opportunities, both of which have a momentous effect on their daily lives. In times of need, the only predictable resources that can be drawn upon are their own children and parents, and the fund of kin and friends obligated to them.

WOMEN AND MEN

"I'm Not in Love with No Man Really"

The emptiness and hopelessness of the job experience for black men and women, the control over meager (AFDC) resources by women, and the security of the kin network, militate against successful marriage or long-term relationships in The Flats. Women and men, nonetheless, begin buoyant new relationships with one another and fall in love, as all races and classes do. But they must wager their relationships against the insurmountable forces of poverty and racism.

The futility of the job experience for street-corner men in a black community is sensitively portrayed by Elliot Liebow in *Tally's Corner*. He writes (1967, p. 63) that "The job fails the man and the man fails the job." Liebow's discussion (1967, p. 142) of men and jobs leads directly to his analysis of the street-corner male's exploitative relationships with women, "Men not only present themselves as economic exploiters of women but they expect other men to do the same." Typical ghetto roles that men try to live up to at home and on the street, and the ghetto man's alleged round-the-clock involvement in peer groups, are interpreted in *Soulside* (Hannerz 1969) as a threat to marital stability. Low-paying menial jobs, unemployment, and welfare regulations, all have powerful, predictable consequences for personal relationships between women and men in The Flats.

Most discussions of sex roles in the black community have looked at interpersonal relationships between women and men from a male point of view.[1] In this chapter social relationships between women and men, mothers and fathers, fathers and children, and men and mothers are seen from a woman's perspective—that is, from the perspective that the women in this study provided, and from my own interpretations of the female scene.

MOTHERS AND FATHERS

When I first met Julia Ambrose she was living in The Flats with her two babies, her cousin Teresa, and Teresa's "old man." After several fierce battles with Teresa over the bills, and her cousin's hostility toward Julia's boyfriends, Julia decided to move. Julia told me she was "head over heels in love with Elliot," her second child's father, and they had decided to live together.

For several months Julia and Elliot shared a small apartment and their relationship was strong. Elliot was very proud of his baby. On weekends he would spend an entire day carrying the baby around to his sister's home and would show it to his friends on the street. Julia, exhilarated by her independence in having her own place, took great care of the house and the children. She told me, "Before Elliot came home from work I would have his dinner fixed and the house and kids clean. When he came home he would take his shower and then I'd bring his food to the bed. I'd put the kids to sleep and then get into bed with him. It was fine. We would get in a little piece and then go to sleep. In the morning we'd do the same thing."

After five months, Elliot was laid off from his job at a factory which hires seasonal help. He couldn't find another job, except part-time work for a cab company. Elliot began spending more time with his friends at the local tavern, and less time with Julia and the children. Julia finally had to get back "on aid' and Elliot put more of his things back in his sister's home so the social worker wouldn't know he was staying with Julia. Juli:

noticed changes in Elliot. "If you start necking and doing the same thing that you've been doing with your man, and he don't want it, you know for sure that he is messing with someone else, or don't want you anymore. Maybe Elliot didn't want me in the first place, but maybe he did, 'cause he chased me a lot. He wanted me and he didn't want me. I really loved him, but I'm not in love with him now. My feelings just changed. I'm not in love with no man really. Just out for what I can get from them."

Julia and Elliot stayed together, but she began to hear rumors about him. Her cousin, a woman who had often expressed jealousy toward Julia, followed Elliot in a car and told her that Elliot parked late at night outside the apartment house of his previous girl friend. Julia told me that her cousin was "nothing but a gossip, a newspaper, who carried news back and forth," and that her cousin was envious of her having an "old man." Nevertheless Julia believed the gossip.

After hearing other rumors and gossip about Elliot, Julia said, "I still really liked him, but I wasn't going to let him get the upper hand on me. After I found out that he was messing with someone else, I said to myself, I was doing it too, so what's the help in making a fuss. But after that, I made him pay for being with me!

"I was getting a check every month for rent from ADC and I would take the money and buy me clothes. I bought my own wardrobe and I gave my mother money for keeping the kids while I was working. I worked here and there while I was on aid and they were paying my rent. I didn't really need Elliot, but that was extra money for me. When he asked me what happened to my check I told him I got cut off and couldn't get back on. My mother knew. She didn't care what I did so long as I didn't let Elliot make an ass out of me. The point is a woman has to have her own pride. She can't let a man rule her. You can't let a man kick you in the tail and tell you what to do.

Anytime I can make an ass out of a man, I'm going to do it. If he's doing the same to me, then I'll quit him and leave him alone."

After Elliot lost his job and kin continued to bring gossip to Julia about how he was playing around with other women, Julia became embittered toward Elliot and was anxious to hurt him. There was a young black man who passed her house every day making deliveries for a local store, and he flirted with her. Charles would slow down his truck and honk for Julia when he passed the house. She started running out to talk to him in his truck and decided to "go" with him. Charles liked Julia and brought nice things for the children.

"I put Elliot in a trick," Julia told me soon after she started going with Charles. "I knew that Elliot didn't care nothing for me so I made him jealous. He was nice to the kids, both of them, but he failed to show me that he was still in love with me. Me and Elliot fought a lot. One night Charles and me went to a motel room and stayed there all night. Mama had the babies. She got mad. But I was trying to hurt Elliot. When I got home, me and Elliot got into it. He called me all kinds of names. I said he might as well leave. But Elliot said he wasn't going nowhere. So he stayed and we'd sleep together, but we didn't do nothing. Then one night something happened. I got pregnant again by Elliot. After I got pregnant, me and Charles quit, and I moved in with a girl friend for a while. Elliot chased after me and we started going back together, but we stayed separate. In my sixth month I moved back in my mother's home with her husband and the kids."

In fact, many women tend to debase men and especially young boys, regarding them as inherently "bad," more susceptible to sin, drinking, going around with women. One older woman told me that men are more evil than women because the serpent—not Eve—tempted Adam, and the serpent was a "he."

Many young women like Julia feel strongly that they cannot

let a man make a fool out of them, and they react quickly and boldly to rumor, gossip, and talk that hurts them. The power that gossip and information plays in constraining the life and duration of sexual relationships is an important cultural phenomenon. But the most important single factor which affects interpersonal relationships between men and women in The Flats is unemployment, and the impossibility for men to secure jobs. Losing a job, or being unemployed month after month, debilitates one's self-importance and independence, and for men, necessitates that they sacrifice their role in the economic support of their families. Thus they become unable to assume the masculine role as defined by American Society.

It is when a man loses his job that he is most likely to begin "messing around." So that no man appears to have made a fool out of them, women respond with vengeance out of pride and self-defense. Another young woman in The Flats, Ivy Rodgers, told me about the time she left her two children in The Flats with her mother and took off for Michigan with Jimmy River, a young man she had fallen in love with "the first sight I seen."

Jimmy asked Ivy to go to Gary, Indiana where his family lived. "I just left the kids with my mama. I didn't even tell her I was going. My checks kept coming, so she had food for the kids. I didn't know he let his people tell him what to do. While we was in Gary Jimmy started messing with another woman. He said he wasn't, but I caught him. I quit him, but when he told me he wasn't messing, I loved him so much that I took him back. Then I got to thinking about it. I had slipped somewhere. I had let myself go. Seems like I forgot that I wasn't going to let Jimmy or any guy make an ass out of me. But he sure was doing it. I told Jimmy that if he loved me, we would go and see my people, take them things, and tell them we were getting married. Jimmy didn't want to go back to The Flats, but I tricked him and told him I really wanted to visit. I picked out my ring and Jimmy paid thirty dollars on it and I had him buy my outfit that we was getting married in. He went along with it. What's so funny was when we come here and he said to me, 'You ready to go back?', I told him, 'No, I'm not going back. I never will marry you.' "

Since the poor in The Flats have learned to rely on kinsmen who cooperate and exchange on a daily basis, and who live near one another or co-reside, women and children find security and support in the domestic network of their kinsmen, and likewise men, young and old, find security in their own kin networks. Kin must intermittently reside with one another. A man's kin may become very jealous and compete for any money he earns, and discourage him from sharing his resources with his girl friends and their children. The incompatibility between the bonds that men and women, girl friends and boyfriends, feel toward one another and the obligations they accept toward their kin also encourage short-lived sexual relationships.

Forms of social control both within the kin network and in the larger society work against successful marriages in The Flats. In fact, couples rarely chance marriage unless a man has a job; often the job is temporary, low paying, insecure, and the worker gets laid off whenever he is not needed. Women come to realize that welfare benefits and ties within kin networks provide greater security for them and their children. In addition, caretaker agencies such as public welfare are insensitive to individual attempts for social mobility. A woman may be immediately cut off the welfare roles when a husband returns home from prison, the army, or if she gets married. Thus, the society's welfare system collaborates in weakening the position of the black male.

Marriage and its accompanying expectations of a home, a job, and a family built around the husband and wife have come to stand for an individual's desire to break out of poverty. It implies the willingness of an individual to remove himself from the daily obligations of his kin network. People in The Flats recognize that one cannot simultaneously meet kin expectations and the expectations of a spouse. While cooperating kinsmen continually attempt to draw new people into their personal networks, they fear the loss of a central, resourceful member in the network. The following passages, taken from a detailed life history of Ruby Banks, show forms of social control working against marriage—forces which effectively maintain kin-based household groupings over the life cycle. Details of her story were substantiated by discussions with her mother, her aunt, her daughter's father, and his sister.

"Me and Otis could be married, but they all ruined that. Aunt Augusta told Magnolia that he was no good. Magnolia was the fault of it too. They don't want to see me married! Magnolia knows that it be money getting away from her. I couldn't spend the time with her and the kids and be giving her the money that I do now. I'd have my husband to look after. I couldn't go where she want me to go. I couldn't come every time she calls me, like if Calvin took sick or the kids took sick, or if she took sick. That's all the running I do now. I couldn't do that. You think a man would put up with as many times as I go over her house in a cab, giving half my money to her all the time? That's the reason why they don't want me married. You think a man would let Aunt Augusta come into the house and take food out of the icebox from his kids? They thought that way ever since I came up.

"They broke me and Otis up. They kept telling me that he didn't want me and that he didn't want the responsibility. I put him out and I cried all night long. And I really did love him. But Aunt Augusta and others kept fussing and arguing, so I went and quit him. I would have got married a long time ago to my first baby's daddy, but Aunt Augusta was the cause of that, telling Magnolia that he was too old for me. She's been jealous of me since the day I was born.

"Three years after Otis I met Earl, Earl said he was going to help pay for the utilities. He was going to get me some curtains and pay on my couch. While Earl was working he was so good to me and my children that Magnolia and them started worrying all over again. They sure don't want me married. The same thing that happened to Otis happened to many of my boy-friends. And I ain't had that many men. I'm tired of them bothering me with their problems when I'm trying to solve my own problems. They tell me that Earl's doing this and that, seeing some girl.

"They look for trouble to tell me every single day. If I ever marry, I ain't listening to what nobody say. I just listen to what he say. You have to get along the best way you know how, and forget about your people. If I got married they would talk, like they are doing now, saying, 'He ain't no good, he's been creep-ing on you. I told you once not to marry him. You'll end up right back on ADC.' If I ever get married, I'm leaving town!"

This passage reveals the strong conflict between kin-based domestic units and lasting ties between husbands and wives. When a mother in The Flats has a relationship with a non-economically productive man, the relationship saps the resources of others in her domestic network. Participants in the network try to break up such relationships in order to maximize their potential resources and the services they hope to exchange. These forms of social control made Ruby afraid to take the risks necessary to break out of the cycle of poverty. Instead, she chose the security and stability of her kin group. Ruby, recognizing that to make a marriage last she would have to move far away from her kin, said, "If I ever get married, I'm leaving town."

While this study was in progress, Ruby did get married, and she left the state with her husband and her youngest child that very evening.

A detailed look at Ruby's life history provides insight into residence strategies during her life. Residence patterns depicted in life histories may clarify the situations which lead to resi-dence changes and domestic alignments, the kin bonds between co-resident adults, and the kin bonds between co-resident adults and children. In the ten years following the birth of Ruby's first child, Ruby and her children frequently exchanged residence and immediate dependencies within a small network of kinsmen. A close look at the sequence of household groupings shows that the same kinsmen are active participants in one another's domestic networks for long periods of time. The following chart shows the sequence of Ruby's changes in residence. The successive recombinations of kinsmen sharing households is represented chronologically.

Ruby Banks and Her Children

Residence History

Age Household Composition and Context of Household Formation

birth *Ruby lived with her mother and her maternal grandparents.*

4 *Ruby and her mother were required to move out of Ruby's grandparents' house so that they could receive AFDC. They moved into a separate residence two houses away, but ate all meals at the grandparents' house.*

5 *Ruby and her mother returned to the grandparents' house and Ruby's mother gave birth to a son. Ruby's mother worked and her grandmother cared for the children.*

6 *Ruby's maternal grandparents separated. Ruby's mother remained living with her father and her two sons (one more born). Ruby and her grandmother moved up the street and lived with her maternal aunt and maternal uncle. Ruby's grandmother took care of Ruby and her brothers, and Ruby's mother worked and cooked and cleaned for her father.*

7–16 *The household now comprised of Ruby, her grandmother, her grandmother's new husband, Ruby's maternal aunt and her boyfriend, Ruby's maternal uncle, and Ruby's younger sister. At age sixteen Ruby gave birth to a daughter.*

17 *Ruby's grandmother died. Ruby had a second child. Ruby remained living with her maternal aunt, her aunt's boyfriend, her maternal uncle, and her two daughters.*

18 *Ruby fought with her aunt. She moved into an apartment with her two daughters. Ruby's first daughter's father died. Her second daughter's father stayed with her and her daughters in the apartment.*

19 *Ruby broke up with the father of her second daughter. Then she and her two daughters joined her mother, her mother's "husband," and her six half-siblings. Ruby had a miscarriage.*

19½ *Ruby left town and moved to out-of-state with her boyfriend. She left her daughters with her mother. She remained there one year, then her mother insisted that she return home and take her children.*

20 *Ruby and her daughters moved into a large house rented by her mother's sister and her mother's brother. It was located next door to her mother's house. Ruby and her children ate at her mother's house. She cleaned for her aunt and uncle. Ruby gave birth to another child.*

21 *Ruby found a house and moved there with her children, her mother's sister, and her mother's sister's boyfriend. Ruby did the cleaning and her aunt cooked. Ruby and her mother, who lived across town, shared child care; Ruby's cousin's daughter stayed with Ruby.*

21½ *Ruby's aunt and boyfriend move out because they are all fighting and they want to get away from the noise of the children. Ruby has a new boyfriend.*

The lack of employment opportunities for the urban poor and unlikeliness of a livable guaranteed minimum income make it very difficult for urban low-income Blacks to form lasting conjugal units. Even if a man and woman set up temporary housekeeping arrangements out of necessity, they continue, as did Ruby, to maintain strong social ties with their kin. Why marriage is unstable is an intricate weave of cause and effect. Kin regard any marriage as both a risk to the woman and her children and as a threat to the durability of the kin group. These two factors continually compete against each other.

FATHERS AND CHILDREN

Although Blacks acquire kin through their mothers and fathers, the economic insecurity of the black male, and the availability of welfare to the female-child unit, makes it difficult for an unemployed black husband-father to compete with a woman's kin for authority and for control over her children.

A father and his kin in The Flats can have a continuing relationship with his children if he has acknowledged paternity, if his kin have activated their claims on the child, and if the mother has drawn these people into her personal network. Usually, the cooperative potential of these people is welcomed, but conflict may arise between kin-based domestic units and lasting ties between husbands and wives. For example, a man's participation is expected in his kin network, and it is assumed that he should not dissipate his services and finances to a sexual or marital relationship.

Although the authority of fathers over their children and their children's mothers is limited, neither the father's interest in his child nor the desire of his kin to help raise a child strains the stability of domestic networks in The Flats. Otis' kin were drawn into Ruby's personal network through his claims on her children and through the long, close friendship between Ruby and Otis' sister, Willa Mae. Like many fathers in The Flats, Otis maintained close contact with his children and provided goods and care for them even when he and Ruby were not on speaking terms. One time when Otis and Ruby separated, Otis stayed in a room in Ruby's uncle's house, which was next door to Ruby's mother's house. At that time Ruby's children were being kept by Magnolia each day while Ruby went to school to finish her high school diploma. Otis was out of work, and he stayed with Ruby's uncle over six months, helping Magnolia care for his children. Otis' kin were proud of the daddy he was, and at times they suggested that they should take over the raising of his and Ruby's children. Ruby and other mothers know well that those people you count on to share in the care and nurturing of your children are also those who are rightfully in the position to judge and check up on how one carries out the duties of a mother. Shared responsibilities of motherhood in The Flats implies both a help and a check on how one assumes a parental role.

Fathers like Otis, dedicated to maintaining ties with their children, learn that the relationship they create with their child's mother largely determines the role they may assume in their child's life. Jealousy between men makes it extremely difficult for fathers to spend time with their children if the mother has a boyfriend, but as Otis said to me, "When Ruby doesn't have any old man, then she starts calling on me, asking for help, and telling me to do something for my kids." In between times, when neither a man nor a woman has a on-going sexual relationship, some mothers call upon the fathers of their children and temporarily "choke" these men with their personal needs and the needs of the children. At these times men and women reinforce their fragile but continuing relationship, and find themselves empathetic friends who can be helpful to one another.

Mothers generally regard their children's fathers as a friends of the family—people they can recruit for help—rather than as a fathers failing in their parental duties. While fathers voluntarily help out their children, many fathers cannot be depended upon as a steady source of income. Claudia Williams, who lives down the street from Lily, talked to me about Raymond, the father of her two children. "Some days he be coming over at night saying, 'I'll see to the babies and you can lay down and rest, honey,' treating me real nice. Then maybe I won't even see him for two or three months. There's no sense nagging Raymond; I just treat him as some kind of friend even if he is the father of my babies." Since Claudia gave birth to Raymond's children both of them have been involved in other relationships. When either of them is involved with someone else, it effectively cuts Raymond off from his children. Claudia says, "My kids don't need their father's help, but if he helps out, then I return the favor. My kids are well behaved and I know they make Raymond's kinfolk proud."

The first time Ruby Banks remembers meeting her father at the market she was about seven years old. She promptly said to him, "Easter's coming, so how about buying me a pair of shoes since you never have given me nothing in your life and you never did nothing for me." By observing their mothers, fathers, and other men and women in The Flats, children learn firsthand how men and women manage one another. They observe goal-oriented behaviors and try them out on each other, on their fathers when they come around, and on their mother's boyfriends. Children are encouraged to profit by any visit from their fathers and his kin, and are rewarded for their gain.

MEN AND MOTHERS

The pride that kinsmen in The Flats take in the children of their sons and brothers is seen best in the pleasure that the mothers and sisters of these men express. Such pride was apparent during a visit I made to Alberta Cox's home. Alberta's husband died when her three children, two sons and a daughter, were young. Since then she has shared a home with her mother, her forty-year-old brother, and her three grown children. When Alberta introduced me to her nineteen-year-old son, she pointed to him and said, "He's a daddy and his baby is four months old." Then she pointed to her twenty-two-year-old son Mac and said, "He's a daddy three times over." Mac smiled and said, "I'm no daddy," and his friend in the kitchen said, "Maybe going on four times, Mac." Alberta said, "Yes you are, admit it, boy!" At that point Mac's grandmother rolled back in her rocker and said, "I'm a grandmother many times over and it make me proud," and Alberta joined her, "Yes, and I'm a grandmother many times over." A friend of Alberta's told me later that Alberta wants her sons to have babies because she thinks it will make them more responsible. Although she does not usually like the women her sons go with, claiming that they are "no good trash," she accepts the babies and asks to care for them whenever she has a chance.

People show pride in all their kin, and particularly new babies born into their kinship networks. Mothers encourage sons to have babies, and even more important, men coax their "old ladies" to have their baby. The value placed on children, the love, attention and affection children receive from women and men, and the web of social relationships spun from the birth of a child are all interlocked in the chain of reproduction and the high birth rate among the poor. The extent to which men coerce women into having their babies is best illustrated by an incident in Rhoda Johnson's life. Rhoda gave birth to her first child when she was fifteen and had three children by the time she was twenty-two. After the birth of her third child Rhoda met Sam, a thirty-five-year-old Flats resident who wanted to marry her. Rhoda, Sam, and the children shared an apartment together through the winter of 1970. One afternoon when I was across the street visiting Rhoda's aunt, Rhoda came into the kitchen very upset. Sam wanted her to have his baby. Rhoda was determined not to have any more children. Sam and his kin in The Flats told Rhoda she ought to have his baby. When the news spread that Rhoda was pregnant no one was surprised. Six or eight weeks later, Rhoda had a miscarriage.

Rhoda was sick in bed when I visited her at her apartment right after the miscarriage. The children were at their aunt's and Sam was out of the house. Rhoda and I had some pop, and she said, "Caroline, I fooled them and I fooled you too. You don't think I was going to have no one's baby. I made up that I was pregnant to get the heat off, and I made up this fool miscarriage too." It was a whole year before Rhoda became pregnant with Sam's baby.

When a young woman in The Flats becomes pregnant with her first child, she and the father do not usually set up house-keeping together in a separate dwelling. Instead, the mother and father remain living in the homes of those kin who raised them. When a mature woman who has several children and a place of her own gives birth, it is very likely that she and her children will rejoin the household of her mother, her sister, or other female kin until she is strong enough to get along on her own. This pattern is brought out in the residence changes of Ruby and her mother, Magnolia.

Women with children have far more economic security than men and women who do not have access to welfare. But forces in the outside society and demands among kin make this security more apparent than real. Welfare regulations encourage mothers to set up separate households, and women want independence, privacy, and an improvement in their lives. But these ventures do not last long. While it might appear to outside observers that there are many single-parent (female-headed) households among low-income Blacks (Moynihan 1965; Bernard 1966), census statistics on female-headed households—on which such studies rely—do not accurately reveal patterns of residence or domestic organization. The life histories of adults show that the attempts by women to set up separate households with their children and husbands, or boyfriends, are short-lived. Lovers fight, jobs are scarce, houses get condemned, and needs for services among kin arise. Ruby's residential changes as a child, and the residences of her own children and kin, reveal that the same factors that contribute to the high frequency of moving in general bring men, women, and children back into the house-holds of close kin. Calamities and crises contribute to the constant shifts in residence. Newly formed households are successive recombinations of the same domestic network of adults and children, quite often in the same dwellings.

Households have shifting membership, but on the average

they maintain a steady state of three generations of kin: males and females beyond childbearing age, a middle generation of mothers raising their own children or children of close kin, and the children. This observation is supported in a recent study by Joyce Ladner (1971, p. 60), who writes, "Many children normally grow up in a three-generation household and they absorb the influences of a grandmother and grandfather as well as [those of] a mother and father." A survey of eighty-three residences changes among AFDC families, whereby adult females who were heads of their own household merged households with other kin, shows that the majority of moves created three-generation households. Consequently it is difficult to pinpoint the structural beginning or end of household cycles in The Flats (Buchler and Selby 1968; Fortes 1958; Otterbein 1970). However, authority patterns within a kin network change with birth and death. With the death of the oldest member in a household, the next generation assumes authority. Ruby's Aunt Augusta acquired dramatic influence over her kin after the grandmother's death. The birth of a child belonging to a new generation recreates a three-generation household after the loss of an elderly member. With this loss and addition, household groupings maintain themselves.

A consequence of the elasticity of residence patterns is that even when persons move to separate households, their social, economic, and domestic lives are so entwined with other kin that they consider themselves simultaneously a part of the residential groupings of their kin. Kin expect to help one another out. That one can repeatedly join the households of kin is a great source of security among those living in poverty, and they come to depend upon it. The loyalties toward kinsmen offset to some degree, the self-defeating ordeal of unemployment and poverty.

8

CONCLUSION

WRITTEN IN COLLABORATION WITH JOHN R. LOMBARDI

Black families in The Flats and the non-kin they regard as kin have evolved patterns of co-residence, kinship-based exchange networks linking multiple domestic units, elastic household boundaries, lifelong bonds to three-generation households, social controls against the formation of marriages that could endanger the network of kin, the domestic authority of women, and limitations on the role of the husband or male friend within a woman's kin network. These highly adaptive structural features of urban black families comprise a resilient response to the social-economic conditions of poverty, the inexorable unemployment of black women and men, and the access to scarce economic resources of a mother and her children as AFDC recipients.

Distinctively negative features attributed to poor families, that they are fatherless, matrifocal, unstable, and disorganized, are not general characteristics of black families living substantially below economic subsistence in urban America. The black urban family, embedded in cooperative domestic exchange, proves to be an organized tenacious, active, lifelong network.

Within domestic networks women and men maintain strong loyalties to their kin, and kin exert internal sanctions upon one another to further strengthen the bond. Attempted social mobility away from the kin network of exchanges and obligations, by means of marriage or employment, involves a precarious risk in contrast to the asylum gained through generosity and exchange. Thus, survival demands the sacrifice of upward mobility and geographic movement, and discourages marriage.

The model of a cooperative life style built upon exchange and reciprocity as described in the present study represents one dimension of the multivalued cultural system, the value-mosaic of the poor. The black urban poor, assuming a cooperative life style, are simultaneously locked into an intimate, ongoing bond with white culture and white values. Employers, social service agencies, mass communication, television, advertising, and teachers and schools continuously reinforce the value system of the traditional middle-class white sector of American society. A single-family home, fine furnishings, and good schools and occupational opportunities for children all constitute values poor Blacks share with mainstream society (see Valentine 1971 for an insightful discussion on this topic). These aspirations can only be realized with accompanying economic opportunity. Consequently, the poor have little opportunity to practice the behaviors associated with affluence.

The value-mosaic of the poor is assembled from a wide range of values from the larger society. Hyman Rodman (1971) has suggested that poor people "stretch" their values in order to cope with poverty. "They share the general values of the society with members of other classes, but in addition they have stretched these values, which help them to adjust to their deprived circumstances" (1971, p. 195). Rodman portrays the value-stretch as a one-way extension, whereby the poor develop a new set of values to cope with deprivation without abandoning the values of mainstream society. Valentine (1971) draws upon the bicultural model to suggest how people are simultaneously enculturated and socialized into their own culture and mainstream culture. Valentine writes that "many Blacks are simultaneously committed to both black culture and mainstream culture, and that the two are not mutually exclusive as generally assumed" (1971, p. 137).

The bicultural model is a powerful social-cultural process by which people learn to appraise immediate or chance opportunity realistically. Biculturation is a stabilizing process by which an individual evaluates the social-economic gains of removing himself from a cooperative kin network (given the possibility of employment) against the security and probable duration of a job. Biculturation is the process by which individuals size up the outcome of hoarding for themselves or sharing with their kin a small sum of money which alone could never improve the standard of living even for a small family. Biculturation furnishes a decision-making model acquired by the experience of poverty. This appraisal mechanism functions as a means of protection, a shield, enabling people to "look before they leap."

The structural adaptations of poverty described in this study do not lock people into a cycle of poverty preventing the poor from marrying, removing themselves from their kin network, or leaving town. But if such opportunities arise (and they rarely do), these chances only are taken after careful evaluation based on both middle-class standards and the experience of poverty. Like many white, middle-class women, black women are likely to evaluate a potential husband in terms of his ability to provide for a family. For example, Julia Ambrose estimated the man she married to be a good provider, a reliable risk. After her husband was laid off his job, Julia was forced to apply for welfare benefits for her children. Ruby Banks returned to The Flats without her husband, within a year of her marriage, embarrassed, disappointed, and depressed. Her pride was injured. She acquired a bitter resentment toward men and toward the harsh conditions of poverty. After the separation, Ruby's husband moved into his older sister's home in a neighboring town. His spirit and optimism toward family life also had been severely weakened.

Many people, politicians, social workers, urban planners,

psychologists, and social scientists, have suggested remedies within the existing social system designed to alleviate poverty, and to provide the poor the opportunity to share in the economic benefits of our affluent society. Programs such as increased educational opportunities, public housing, a negative income tax and welfare reform have been proposed. These programs appear to be designed to increase social-economic mobility. Such programs are doomed to failure. This is because within our economic system these inequities are not unfortunate accidents. They are necessary for the maintenance of the existing economic order.

Two necessary requirements for ascent from poverty into the middle class are the ability to form a nuclear family pattern, and the ability to obtain an equity. Close examination of the welfare laws[1] and policies relating to public assistance show that these programs systematically tend to reduce the possibility of social mobility. Attempts by those on welfare to formulate nuclear families are efficiently discouraged by welfare policy. In fact, welfare policy encourages the maintenance of non-coresidential cooperative domestic networks. It is impossible for potentially mobile persons to draw all of their kin into the middle class. Likewise, the welfare law conspires against the ability of the poor to build up an equity. Welfare policy effectively prevents the poor from inheriting even a pitifully small amount of cash, or from acquiring capital investments typical for the middle class, such as home ownership.

It is clear that mere reform of existing programs can never be expected to eliminate an impoverished class in America. The effect of such programs is that they maintain the existence of such a class. Welfare programs merely act as flexible mechanisms to alleviate the more obvious symptoms of poverty while inching forward just enough to purchase acquiescence and silence on the part of the members of this class and their liberal supporters. As we have seen, these programs are not merely passive victims of underfunding and conservative obstructionism. In fact they are active purveyors of the status quo, staunch defenders of the economic imperative that demands maintenance of a sizable but docile impoverished class.

One might be tempted to ask of what value the existence of a class of unemployed and unskilled, but costly individuals could possibly be to the maintenance of our present economic system (see Piven and Cloward 1971). The answer lies partly in the utility of having a large pool of unemployed readily available to be absorbed into the work force in times of rapid economic expansion. Further, and perhaps more important, the existence of a large pool of unemployed people puts pressure on those employed in the lower income brackets and on most of the unskilled positions within the labor force. The ready availability of replacements decreases their job security and reduces the possibility that they will demand higher wages. The willingness of this employed but insecure and underpaid group in turn puts pressure on those in the next higher category of skills and pay who are always ready to displace them. This process continues on up the scale of skills and salary so that even the unskilled and unemployed contribute to holding down wages throughout the lower economic strata in our society.

People in The Flats have acquired a remarkably accurate assessment of the social order in American society. For example, they can realistically appraise the futility of hoarding a small cash reserve such as life insurance benefits or a temporary increase in cash available to a kin network by means of the employment of a network member. Such short-lived gains are quickly redistributed among members of a kin network. Kinsmen, inclined to share their luck, provide a model of cooperative behavior for others in the community. What is seen by some interpreters as disinterest in delayed rewards is actually a rational evaluation of need.

Mainstream values have failed many residents of The Flats.

Nevertheless, the present study shows that the life ways of the poor present a powerful challenge to the notion of a self-perpetuating culture of poverty. The strategies that the poor have evolved to cope with poverty do not compensate for poverty in themselves, nor do they perpetuate the poverty cycle. But when mainstream values fail the poor, as they have failed most Flats' residents, the harsh economic conditions of poverty force people to return to proven strategies for survival.

APPENDIXES

Appendix A

AFDC Case History Survey

The AFDC case history survey is a statistical study of kinship and residence patterns from 188 case records of black recipients of AFDC in the county in which this study was made. The study includes data on 951 children who are AFDC recipients —half of the total number of AFDC children in the county in 1969—and 373 adults, of whom 188 were "grantees" responsible for the AFDC child.

My objective in using the AFDC case files was to become acquainted with a broad spectrum of AFDC families and to be exposed to the biases of the social workers' definitions of the "problems" confronting these families.

The files included fact sheets containing statistical data on the names, ages, and place of birth of grantees and their children, and long, detailed and highly personalized comments written by case workers over the years. The oldest case records contained information on some of the first families to become ADC recipients in the late thirties. They were thick records of two and sometimes three generations of welfare recipients within one family.

In the process of reading at least one hundred case histories, I began to search for the kind of data which appeared consistently in each of the case histories and which appeared to be reliable data (some of course was not). I drew up about two hundred questions on information in the case histories on adults and children. These questions were coded on a trial basis by two trained assistants so that we could clarify the assumptions we held for each question and write a list of instructions for coding.

A program (Fortran is part of the general system) was designed to analyze the data which was coded and punched on call cards. In order to attain coder reliability, the coders randomly selected one out of every five cases and cross-coded so that assumptions could be compared for any differences in coding.

The following are drafts of the information that were coded on grantees, other adults in the household, and children in the case histories.

I THE GRANTEE

DRAFT OF CODING SYSTEM FOR ADC CASES

CARD 1: THE GRANTEE

COLUMN #	TITLE OF COLUMN AND ITS CODE
1,2,3	*Case Number*
	Begin 001, 002, etc.
4	*Card Number*
	Code 1
5	*Type of Case*
	1. ADC.
	2. ADCU.
6,7	*Year (19—) of date of first application of present grantee*
8	*Sex of grantee*
	1. Female.
	2. Male.
9,10	*Birth date of grantee (19—)*
	00. Not ascertained.
11,12	*Birthplace of grantee*

SOUTH	CENTRAL	MOUNTAIN
01. Kentucky	19. Ohio	40. Montana
02. Tennessee	20. Indiana	41. Wyoming
03. Alabama	21. Illinois	42. Idaho
04. Mississippi	22. Michigan	43. Colorado
05. Arkansas	23. Wisconsin	44. Arizona
06. Louisiana	24. Minnesota	45. Utah
07. Oklahoma	25. Iowa	46. Nevada
08. Texas	26. Missouri	
09. Delaware	27. No. Dakota	PACIFIC
10. Maryland	28. So. Dakota	47. Washington
11. District of	29. Nebraska	48. Orgeon
Columbia	30. Kansas	49. California
12. Virginia		50. Hawaii
13. W. Virginia	ATLANTIC	51. Alaska
14. No. Carolina	31. New York	52. Unknown
15. So. Carolina	32. New Jersey	53. In service
16. Georgia	33. Pennsylvania	54. Dead
17. Florida	34. Maine	
18. New Mexico	35. New Hampshire	
	36. Vermont	
	37. Massachusetts	
	38. Rhode Island	
	39. Connecticut	

13   Birthplace of grantee by geographic area

0. Not ascertained
1. South (if 11, 12 was 01–17)
2. Central (18–29)
3. Atlantic (30–38)
4. Mountain (39–45)
5. Pacific (46–49)

14   Number of rooms in household up to date

0. Not ascertainable.
1–8
9. Nine or more.

15   *Number of individuals in household up to date*
0. Not ascertainable.
1–8
9. Nine or more.

16   *Number of ADC children in household under 18*
up to date (include a minor ADC mother)
0. Not ascertainable.
1–8
9. Nine or more.

17   *Number of adult males in household over 18 up to date*
0. None.
1–8
9. Nine or more.

18   *Number of children in household under 18*
(ADC plus others) up to date
1–8
9. Nine or more.

19   *Number of adult females in household over 18*
up to date, including mothers
0. None.
1–8
9. Nine or more.

20   *Total number of spouses (wives, husbands, common*
law, etc.) of grantee as far as case history goes
0. None.
1–8
9. Nine or more.

21   *Total number of fathers in the case history that the*
female grantee lists as fathers of all these children
(she may not be the mother). Rule: Make an intelligent
guess when possible.
0. Not applicable or not ascertainable.
1–8
9. Nine or more.

22   *Is the grantee's spouse (or ex-spouse) a member of the*
household up to date (include common law, etc.)

0. *Not ascertainable or not applicable.*
1. *Yes.*
2. *No.*
3. *Sometimes.*
4.
5.

23   *If yes to #22, what is the relationship of spouse to grantee?*
0. *Not relevant.*
1. *Legally married.*
2. *Common law (stated as such).*
3. *Free union (living together for less than seven years).*
4. *Marriage annulled.*
5.
6.
7.
8.
9.

24   *Number of spouse units (common law, etc.) in the household up to date*
0. *None.*
1–8
9. *Nine or more.*

25   *Number of single mother/child units in the household up to date. ("Single" means that there is no husband/father for this unit in the household.)*
0. *None.*
1–8
9. *Nine or more.*

26   *Number of father/child units in this household up to date. ("Unit" means a father and all his children.)*
0. *None.*
1–8
9. *Nine or more.*

27   *Number of stepfather/child units in this household up to date. ("Unit" means a stepfather and all his children.)*
0. *None.*

	1–8
	9. *Nine or more.*
28,29	*From the time of application, if the grantee has ever changed his/her household unit to join or be joined by another relative's household, what is the relationship between the grantee and the adult heads of the new household which they joined or merged with? Code for first move.*
	Master Code: Relationship
30,31	*Same as 28,29 for second move, use Master Code.*
32,33	*Same as 28,29 for third move, use Master Code.*
34	*Is there a 3" x 5" card on this case which summarizes residence facts that I should read or notes an interesting aspect of this case?*
	1. *Yes.*
	2. *No.*
35,36	*Relation of grantee to "responsible relative"*
	listed first on list
39,40	*(listed 2nd)*
43,44	*(listed 3rd)*
47,48	*(listed 4th)*
51,52	*(listed 5th)* **Master Code: Relationships**
55,56	*(listed 6th)*
59,60	*(listed 7th)*
63,64	*(listed 8th)*
67,68	*(listed 9th)*
71,72	*(listed 10th)*
75,76	*(listed 11th)*
37,38	*Location of responsible relative coded above at time of application*
41,42	*2nd*
45,46	*3rd*
49,50	*4th*
53,54	*5th* **Master Code: Places 1, 11, 12**
57,58	*6th*
61,62	*7th*

65,66	8th
69,70	9th
73,74	10th
77,78	11th
79,80	Relationship of grantee to migrant or temporary resident in household, or relationship of grantee to person sharing kitchen, bath, or meals. (Pick first visitor mentioned who stayed for a while.)

Relationships: Master Code

00. *Not ascertainable, not relevant*

Consanguines

Female	Male	Kin term used
01. *Mo*	18. *Fa*	35. *Aunt*
02. *MoMo*	19. *FaFa*	36. *Uncle*
03. *FaMo*	20. *MoFa*	37. *Niece or Nephew*
04. *FaFaSi*	21. *FaBr*	38. *Grandniece*
05. *MoFaSi*	22. *MoBr*	39. *Half Sibling*
06. *FaSi*	23. *FaFaBr*	40. *Grandnephew*
07. *MoSi*	24. *MoFaBr*	41. *Granddaughter*
08. *Si*	25. *Br*	42. *Grandson*
09. *Da*	26. *So*	43. *Stepmother*
10. *DaDa*	27. *DaSo*	44. *Stepfather*
11. *SoDa*	28. *SoSo*	45. *Stepchild*
12. *BrDa*	29. *SiSo*	46. *Stepmother's family*
13. *SiDa*	30. *BrSo*	47. *Stepfather's family*
14. *FaBrDa*	31. *FaBrSo*	48. *Great-grandchild*
15. *FaSiDa*	32. *FaSiSo*	49. *grantee marries*
16. *MoBrDa*	33. *MoBrSo*	
17. *MoSiDa*	34. *MoSiSo*	

Affines—In-laws, Relatives by Marriage

Female	Male	
50. *Wife*	73. *Husband*	93. *01 and 18*
51. *HuMo*	74. *HuFa*	94. *91 and 42, 44*

52. WiMo
53. HuBrWi
54. WiBrWi
55. HuSi
56. WiSi
57. SoWi
58. BrWi
59. HuMoBrWi
60. WiMoBrWi
61. HuFaMo
62. WiFaMo
63. HuFaBrSoWi
64. WiFaBrSoWi
65. HuSiDa
66. WiSiDa
67. HuBrDa
68. WiBrDa
69. FaBrSoWi
70. SoSoWi
71. FaBrWi
72. MoBrWi

75. WiFa
76. HuBr
77. WiBr
78. DaHu
79. SiHu
80. HuMoBr
81. WiMoBr
82. HuFaBrSo
83. WiFaBrSo
84. HuSiSo
85. WiSiSo
86. HuBrSo
87. WiBrSo
88. FaSiDaHu
89. SoDaHu
90. MoSiHu
91. FaSiHu
92. 02 and 20

95. 08 and 79
96. 25 and 58
97. 09 and 78
98. None of these
99. Non-Kin

Hint:
 mo=mother
 fa=father
 wi=wife
 hu=husband
 si=sister
 br=brother
 da=daughter
 so=son

II CHILDREN

DRAFT OF CODING SYSTEM FOR ADC CASES

CARDS 2 AND 3: DATA ON CHILDREN

COLUMN #	TITLE OF COLUMN AND ITS CODE
1,2,3	Case Number
	Begin 001, 002, 003.
4	Card Number
	Code 2 or 3 or 4.
5,6	Child's birth date (19—) (Serves as identification.)
23,24	00. No data for this card.
41,42	01. Unknown.

59,60	
7	Sex of child being coded
25	1. Male.
43	2. Female.
61	3. Unknown.
8	Is child being coded currently on ADC?
26	1. Yes.
44	2. No.
62	0. Not ascertainable.
9	Is child being coded currently in the grantee's household?
27	0. Not ascertainable.
45	1. Yes.
63	2. No.
	3. No further data.
10,11	Child's birthplace
28,29	Code as Card 1, 11, 12.
46,47	
64,65	
12,13	Relationship of child to grantee from grantee's point of view. (Grantee is EGO.)
30,31	Master Code: Relationships
48,49	
66,67	
14	Are child's parents in grantee's household up to date?
32	0. Not ascertainable.
50	1. No.
68	2. Mother is in household.
	3. Father is in household.
	4. Stepfather is in household.
	5. 2 and 3.
	6. 2 and 4.
	7. Stepmother is in household.
	8. 4 and 7.
	9. 3 and 7.
15	Location of biological mother of child
	Code these in the order listed.

33	0. *Not ascertainable.*
51	1. *Not applicable.*
69	2. *In household.*
	3. *In Jackson Harbor.*
	4. *In Chicago.*
	5. *In Gary.*
	6. *In Illinois other than above.*
	7. *In the South.*
	8. *Other.*
	9. *Dead.*
16	If the mother is not the grantee, *what is the status of the mother of the child up to date?* Code these in the order listed.
34	0. *Not applicable.*
52	1. *Unmarried minor in household.*
70	2. *Married minor in household.*
	3. *Unmarried adult in household.*
	4. *Married adult in household.*
	5. *She deserted this child.*
	6. *She is divorced and living elsewhere.*
	7. *She is divorced and in the household.*
	8. *She is an adult living outside the household.*
	9. *None of these.*
17,18	*If the child moves out of grantee's household,*
35,36	*what is the relationship between the child being*
53,54	*coded and the adult heads of the new household?*
71,72	*("Household head" means the responsible adults in the household.)*
	Code the relationship from the child's point of view.
	Master Code: Relationships
19	*Status of biological father of child*
37	0. *Not ascertainable.*
55	1. *Legal father.*
73	2. *Putative father.*
	3. *Unknown father.*
	4. *Marriage annulled.*

5. Dead.

6.

7.

20   *Does grantee imply that the biological father of this child has admitted to fathering the child (like he paid the hospital bill or intended to)? (Code impression before decision is made at court hearing.)*

38   1. Not ascertainable.

56   2. Yes.

74   3. No, she implies that he denied it.

21   *Source of support (full or partial) for child being coded*

39   1. Father of child where father lives in the household.

57   2. Father of child where father lives outside the household.

75   3. Stepfather who lives in the household.

     4. Stepfather who lives outside household.

     5. Mother who lives in the household.

     6. Mother working who lives outside household.

     7. None.

     8. Other.

     9. Not ascertainable.

22   *How long has this child been a member of the grantee's household?*

40   0. Not ascertainable.

58   1. Less than a month.

76   2. Less than a year.

     3. 1–3 years.

     4. 4–6 years.

     5. 7–10 years.

     6. 10 years or more.

77   *Female adult relatives who were on ADC*

     0. Not ascertainable.

     1. Mo.

     2. MoMo.

     3. MoSi.

     4. FaMo.

     5. FaSi.

6. *1 and 2.*
7. *1 and 4.*
8. *2 and 4.*
9. *Other.*

III   ADULTS

DRAFT OF CODING SYSTEM FOR ADC CASES

CARD 4: DATA ON ADULTS (OTHER THAN THE GRANTEE) WHO ARE LIVING IN THE HOUSEHOLD OR WHO HAVE LIVED IN THE GRANTEE'S HOUSEHOLD

COLUMN #	TITLE OF COLUMN AND ITS CODE
1,2,3	*Case Number* *Begin 001, 002, 003.*
4	*Card Number* *Code 5.*
5	*Is there data on this card?* *0. No.* *1. Yes.*
6	*Sex of adult (over 18). Code any adult other than*
13	*grantee who is currently residing in the same*
20	*household as the grantee or who has resided there*
27	*since the date of application. Code according to the*
34	*chronological order. (Include ADC turned 18.)*
41	*0.*
48	*1. Female who has ever been an ADC child*
55	*on this grantee's case.*
62	*2. Male who has ever been an ADC child*
69	*on this grantee's case.*
	3. Female not an ADC child on this grantee's case.
	4. Male not an ADC child on this grantee's case.
7,8	*Date of birth of adult being coded (19——)*
14,15	*00. Not ascertainable.*
21,22	*01. Born in 1899 or 1900.*

28,29
35,36
42,43
49,50
56,57
63,64
70,71

9,10   *Relationship of grantee to adult being coded*
16,17   *(take grantee as person*
23,24   *stating the relationship).*
30,31   *Code—Master Code: Relationships*
37,38
44,45
51,52
58,59
65,66
72,73

11   *Does the adult have any children or stepchildren*
         in this household?
18   *0. Not ascertainable.*
25   *1. No.*
32   *2. One son.*
39   *3. One daughter.*
46   *4. Two children.*
53   *5. Three children.*
60   *6. Four children.*
67   *7. Five children.*
74   *8. Six children or more.*
12   *How long was this adult a member of the grantee's*
19   *household? (fairly continuously)*
26   *0. Not ascertainable or relevant.*
33   *1. Less than a month.*
40   *2. Less than a year.*
47   *3. 1–3 years.*
54   *4. 4–6 years.*
61   *5. 7–10 years.*
68   *6. 10 years or more.*

Appendix B

Outline of Interview Topics

A. SOCIAL AND DOMESTIC RELATIONS

1. DAILY LIVES

Comment: This interview is hard to do unless you know the person really well. The aim is to learn how people spend their time from the moment they wake up in the morning until they go to bed at night. We are trying to learn who they visit, which relatives they see daily or weekly, what they do for each other, whether they exchange goods and services, and how these exchanges are arranged.

a. Ask the person to describe a typical day in great detail. Help them along by asking detailed questions.

b. Who does the person visit each day, each week? Which relatives (relationship), boyfriends, friends, fathers of their children, etc.

c. Did they trade clothes, money, child care with anyone this week? With whom?

d. What did they do for someone else this week? Did anyone help them out?

e. What guys (girls) do they see each week (not names); for example, fathers, boyfriends, mothers of their children, sisters, etc.

f. Do they give to any of the individuals listed in *e*? Do they receive money from any of the individuals listed in *e*?

2. THE ACQUISITION OF GOODS

Comment: Ask the person to name all of the items (furniture, pictures, radios, etc.) in each room in their house. Give each item a number and ask the following questions about each item.

a. Give a physical description of the item.
b. How long has it been in the house?
c. Was the item in anyone else's home before? Whose?
d. Does it belong to anyone in the house? Who?
e. Where did it come from? Was it bought at a store? Where?
f. Was it bought for cash, credit?
g. Was it bought new or used?
h. Who bought it?
i. Who made the decision to buy it?
j. How much did it cost?
k. Was it a gift or a loan?
l. Who loaned or gave it to you?
m. Who will it be given to or loaned to?
n. Is it home-made? Who made it?
o. What else should we ask you about it?

3. FINANCES

Comment: Everyone has a hard time making it on the money they get and so you have to get some help from others. The aim is to try to figure out how people make it financially, how their daily and weekly budget works. This gets very complicated because some people live together, others eat together, and others share their income.

a. Learn who is living in the house of the person you are interviewing (list relationships) and how they contribute to the finances of the household (rent, utilities, food, etc.).
b. Who eats in the household? Which meals? Who pays for the food? Who cooks?
c. Try to learn the source of income of everyone in the household and how much they earn (you may have to guess).
d. Learn other ways people in the house get money and the amount; for example, from boyfriends, children's fathers, parents, etc.
e. Try to write down a complete budget which includes how much money comes into the house and from where, expenses, who pays for what.

4. LEISURE TIME AND SEX ROLES

Comment: Men and women have leisure time to spend and finances to organize. We are trying to learn who people spend their free time with, and the differences between men and women's buying habits.

a. In whose name are the insurance policies?

b. In whose name is the car, the house?

c. Does your wife or girl friend (husband, boyfriend) buy your clothes, or do you buy your own?

d. Where do you sleep, keep your clothes, records?

e. Where and with whom do you eat breakfast, lunch, dinner?

f. How and with whom do you spend your day?

g. Which bills do you pay?

h. What housework do you do (shopping, scrubbing, cooking, dishes, etc.)?

i. When and how much time do you spend with your own children? Your nieces and nephews?

B. GOSSIP

1. How do you keep up on what's happening to people you don't see very often?

2. Who do you gossip with?

3. How much time do people spend gossiping? How much time did you spend gossiping this week? Give an example.

4. What is the difference between gossip and when someone comes over to your house and says to you, "Your man's creeping on you?" What do you call something that someone tells you to your face but is not true?

5. What do people gossip about? Give examples.

6. Do you learn anything about how people should act from gossiping?

7. What is the difference between what people gossip about in front of a person or behind his back?

8. How much do people believe gossip?

9. How does gossip spread? If you tell a friend something, how long would it take for your mother to hear about it?

10. How many people gossip together at a time? Who, if anyone, is left out of the group?

11. What kind of people do people gossip about the most? What do they say?

12. What makes a person a good gossiper? How do these people get their information?

13. Why do people gossip?

C. KINSHIP AND RESIDENCE

1. WHO ARE YOUR RELATIVES?

Comment: The study of American kinship has left many unknowns. Students of black kinship do not have an agreed-upon American kinship model that they can compare to black kinship. Some of the unknowns in the study of American kinship that are of interest in the study of black kinship are the following:

a. In the black community, who is considered to be a relative or kin? Who counts as kin? There are many possibilities: blood relatives on the mother's side, the father's side, or both; in-laws; friends.

b. In order to get at this very basic question, you have to be very "open-ended." You can't make the mistake of giving people answers, or examples, because they catch on very quickly to the kind of answers you want.

c. Begin by asking the question, "Do you have any relatives?"

d. If the answer is yes, then ask, "Who are your relatives?"

e. List the names the informant gives. Have him/her look at the list and decide whether he/she wants to add anyone to the list. At this point don't say, "Well, does Joe have a brother, a wife, kids?" You want to get their own view of who their relatives are without prompting them or helping out.

f. After you have the list of names, then find out the relationship of each person to the informant. You will end up with a list of kin-types (daughter, mother, father, etc) and non-kin types, friends, etc.

g. At this point you know how many relatives are listed, the order in which they were given, the kin types listed on the informant's mother's and father's side, which includes kin terms like *step, great, grand,* etc. When these terms appear, find out what they mean; for example, what is a grandnephew?.

h. For each person listed, find out what the informant calls the person.

2. THE BASIC GENEALOGY

Comment: In contrast to "Who are your relatives?", when you gather the informant's genealogy, you want to push as far as you can to get the informant to list every blood relative and relative by marriage that he can possibly remember. Even if the informant can't remember names, if he is aware of a great-grandfather who had six brothers, put these down on the chart. The purpose of gathering this extensive list of kin is so that you can eventually gather all sorts of genealogical information (residence, employment, etc.) about the relative. The easiest way to start is to begin with the informant's (Ego) own generation and work down, because these people are freshest in his mind. Once he catches on, then you can work upwards to his parents' generation and grandparents' generation. (Ego refers to informant.)

a. Ego's Generation: Write down the names of Ego's brothers and sisters.

   i. Write down the name of Ego's children and the names of his brothers' and sisters' children.

   ii. Write down the names of all of Ego's children's fathers/mothers. Elicit the relationship of Ego to the parent of each child.

   iii. Write down the names of Ego's siblings' children, the children's fathers/mothers, and the relationship of those parents to Ego's brothers and sisters.

   iv. Write down any additional spouses or consensual unions of Ego and Ego's siblings that are not already included.

   v. For each of Ego's partners (spouse, consensual union, parent to Ego's child), get their brothers, sisters, parents, grandparents, etc., and repeat ii–iv for each of them.

b. Ego's Children's Generation:

   i. For each of Ego's children, and for Ego's siblings' children, repeat ii–v. To do this, consider each child as Ego when you are asking the questions. This way you can learn about half siblings.

c. Ego's Parents' Generation:

i. Write down Ego's mother's and father's name, and the names of all the children born to each.

ii. Write the relationship between Ego's parents and the parents of any children they had with another partner.

iii. Write down any additional spouses or consensual unions of Ego's parents that are not already included.

iv. For each of Ego's parents' siblings (do one side at a time), repeat i–iii for all children born to them and to additional partnerships.

d. Ego's Parents' Parents:

i. Repeat (c) i–iv for Ego's mother's mother, mother's father, father's mother, and father's father.

3. GENEALOGICAL INFORMATION

a. For each relative in the genealogy, gather the following information: age, sex, relationship to Ego, whether living or dead, place of birth, current place of residence, major occupation or source of income, total number of spouses, total number of consensual unions, total number of children, education, whether rents or owns home, year and cause of death.

4. RESIDENCE LIFE HISTORIES: CHILDREN

Comment: The following data will eventually be gathered for everyone in the genealogy, but for now the emphasis is on children in the genealogy (informant's children's generation) because the informant's memory is best at this level. The focus of this data is where and with whom these children lived as they were growing up. Much of this information constitutes details in the life histories, but at this point the emphasis is on residence and the specific changes in the residence of children. For each child we are interested in straightforward data on residence changes and in rules about the decision-making process. Gather data for each child from birth to the present.

a. Name of child.

b. Relationship of child to informant: state relationships from informant's point of view; for example, the informant's sister's daughter. For comparison with the computer study, be sure and keep point of view clear.

c. Age at time of move.

d. For each change in residence since birth, get the following information:

    i. Relationship of child to adult male in new household: state relationship from point of view of child.

    ii. Relationship of child to adult female in new household: state relationship from point of view of child.

Note: For i and ii, take "adult" to mean responsible adults in household. If a child moved to a household and the informant says he moved to "my sister's house," write down that relationship for ii even if the sister's mother and others are also in the household. When in doubt, write down more than one response for i and ii.

e. Other relatives in household.

f. Location of household (city and state).

g. Reason for move: Ask informant to describe the situation in which the change took place. (Eventually we will have this information from several points of view.)

h. Who made the decision?

i. What alternatives were open? What other relatives were considered? Non-kin?

5. RESIDENCE LIFE HISTORIES: ADULTS

Comment: Begin with the adults in the informant's genealogies (Ego and his siblings) and work upwards in the genealogy to great-grandparents, etc., on both sides. Basically we want the same data that is gathered for children, but the adult residence charts might be more sketchy as you get to older and more distant kin. For each adult, gather the following data from birth to the present, or to the death of the individual.

a. Name of adult.

b. Relationship to informant from informant's point of view.

c. Age at time of move. Year of move.

d. Location of household (city, state). This information gives us a picture of migration, where they moved, when, who joined whom, etc.

e. Relationship to adult male in new household: state relationship from point of view of person whose life you are detailing.

f. Relationship of adult female in new household: state relationship from point of view of person whose life you are detailing.

g. Other relatives in that specific household.

h. Other relatives living in the general area near household (especially if this move is part of migration).

i. Reason for the move.

j. Who made the decision?

k. What alternatives were open (other places to move, other relatives to join)?

D. CHILD-KEEPING AND FOSTERAGE

Comment: For each example of extended child-keeping or fosterage (over six months) found in the Residence Life Histories of Children, get the following information wherever possible.

1. DECISION MODEL

a. Who was involved in making the decision?

b. What is their relationship to the child?

c. How was the decision made?

d. Events surrounding the decision.

e. What possible alternatives were considered?

f. How long has the child lived in household? What were the original intentions?

g. What rights have the male and female in the household acquired over the child? What rights do they not have?

· 2. THE MOTHER

a. Number of children she has living with her.

b. Marital status, economic status.

    c. Social relationship of fathers of her children to children living with her.

3. THE CHILD

    a. Age, place in family he was born into (oldest, youngest).

    b. Residential history: Has the child been "kept" before? By whom?

    c. Social relationship to his biological father.

    d. Social relationship to his biological mother, siblings.

    e. Kin map: Which adults does the child consider to be his relatives?

    f. What does a child call adults in household and his biological parents? How does he refer to them?

Notes

Introduction

1. This approach has been labeled "ethnomethodology" or the "naturalistic method." The aim of field work to the ethnomethodologist is to reduce the distance between the model an outsider uses to explain social order, and the constructs employed by those studied (see Cicourel 1964; Denzin 1970; Strauss 1959).

2. Black Urban Poor

1. I am grateful to a number of friends and colleagues for helpful discussions on the "culture of poverty" at various stages of this research. I would like to thank Peter Hainer, Douglas Midgett, Shelton Davis, and John Lombardi. I am also grateful to participants in the Fourth World Seminar at Boston University.

2. Between 1935 and 1939 most states adopted legislation to make use of categorical grants-in-aid. States were slow to implement categorical assistance programs for dependent children (AFDC) and by December 1940 only 360,000 had been put on the nation's AFDC rolls (see Piven and Cloward 1971; Steiner 1971). AFDC was first called Aid to Dependent Children (ADC) but was later renamed Aid to Families with Dependent Children (AFDC). I shall use AFDC in the text to this study, although many of the people quoted throughout the study still refer to the program as "ADC."

3. On the basis of field research in the West Indies and the United States, R. T. Smith (1970) formulated some important hypotheses regarding black family organization. He suggests that "there are differences in the normative structure of familial relations and these differences distinguish lower- from middle-class family structure irrespective of whether household composition is the same or is different" (1970, p. 60). Smith's work constitutes a major contribution to our understanding of the normative

kinship system of Afro-Americans. His suggestions which lend support to hypotheses in this study are the following: (1) lower-class kinship lacks the ideological and normative emphasis upon the isolated nuclear family; (2) lower-class persons continue to be involved with other kin even if they live in a nuclear family; (3) household boundaries are elastic; (4) there exist clusters of close-female kin constituting cooperating groups; (5) there is a tendency to keep as many kinship links open as possible; (6) transactions of mutual help are not confined to the bounds of a nuclear family unit.

Smith has suggested the existence of cooperative groups extending beyond the nuclear family. I expressed a similar view of the black family (Stack 1970, p. 311), suggesting that participants in domestic units of cooperation align to provide the basic functions often attributed to nuclear family units. Smith's work is a fundamental step toward our understanding of the normative structure of lower-class families, but his analysis does not shed light on how the structure works in daily life. Although he recognizes that kin help one another, he concludes that "this is not to say that one finds large, co-operating groups of kinsfolk among the lower class (1971, p. 68)...." In contrast, this study demonstrates the stability and collective power of cooperative kinsmen even among the poorest black families in The Flats.

3. Swapping: "What Goes Round Comes Round"

1. Foster's (1963) model of the dyadic contract includes two types of dyadic contractual ties: colleague ties between individuals of approximately equal socio-economic positions and patron-client ties between individuals of unequal social position. The underlying principles of exchange transactions discussed in this chapter approximate features of the dyadic model of colleague ties. According to Foster's model, colleague ties are expressed by repeated exchanges; they are informal and exist as long as participants are satisfied; they are usually of long duration; and exact or perfectly balanced reciprocity between partners is never achieved.

2. "Essential kin" refers to members of the culturally specific system of kinship categories and others who activate and validate their jural rights by helping one another, thereby creating reciprocal obligations toward one another (see Chapter 4). Firth (1970) distinguishes between "effective kin" (those kin with whom one maintains social contact) and "intimate kin" (those kin with whom contact is purposeful, close, and frequent—members of the immediate family circle.).

4. Personal Kindreds: "All Our Kin"

1. Schneider (1968) maintains that distinctions between terms of reference (father) and terms of address (pa, pop, daddy) increase ethnographic error because they are synonyms which are equally referential and are equally names of categories. Schneider's observation clearly is not adequate for dealing with the terminology from the above passage. The kinship term *father* in the passage refers to the *socially recognized genitor*. "Daddy," which informants themselves put in quotations by intonation, refers to an essential kin such as the man who raises a child. Black people in The Flats, then, distinguish between the "pater" (essential kin), the jural father (the socially recognized genitor), and the "genitor." This perception of fatherhood does not fit into the long-accepted dichotomy between "pater" and "genitor" (Radcliffe-Brown 1950).

2. The following distinction between relatives, kin, and essential kin will be used throughout the study: (a) *relatives*: in cognatic reckoning the universe of cognates is in principle unlimited in the number of genealogical categories (not persons) it contains. A relative is any person who is genealogically defined within the cognatic web; (b) *kin*: some relatives (at least) and some others who are members of the culturally specific system of kinship categories which have behavioral entailments with respect to one another; (c) *essential kin*: at least some of the above kin and others who activate and validate their jural rights by helping one another, thereby creating reciprocal obligations toward one another.

3. I wish to thank Ward Goodenough for clarifying this point, and for other valuable suggestions.
4. I am grateful to Jan Brukman for suggesting this idea.
5. On this point in particular, and many others throughout this chapter, I wish to thank F. K. Lehman.
6. Professor Charles Valentine and Betty Lou Valentine provided extensive comments on this chapter at an early stage in the writing. I am extremely grateful for their generous help and criticism.

5. Child-Keeping: "Gimme a Little Sugar"

1. Child-keeping corresponds to the general characterizations of fosterage (Carroll 1970; Goody 1966; Keesing 1970a; Sanford 1971). Keesing (1970a) and Sanford (1971) have defined fosterage as the housing of a dependent child in a household which does not include the mother or father. Carroll (1970) views fostering in more specific terms as a temporary obligation of kinsmen to take care of one another's children. Goody (1966) contrasts kinship fostering in crisis situations with the rights of kinfolk to take children and rear them apart from their own parents.
2. Residence life histories are detailed chronological accounts of the residence changes from birth to the present. For each residence change or change in household composition, I gathered data on: (1) the age of the person at the time of each residence change; (2) the situation which precipitated the move (context); and (3) the kinship links between members of each newly formed household (see Appendix B).
3. This section reflects theoretical advances in the analysis of transactions in parenthood (Goodenough 1970) and role analysis (Goodenough 1965; Keesing 1969, 1970a, 1970b), and stimulating discussions with Douglas Midgett and Norma Linton who are both engaged in research on patterns of child exchange.
4. Rivers (1924) makes a strikingly similar statement in his book *Social Organization*. He says that "A child born into a com-

munity with societies or clans becomes a member of a domestic group other than the family in the strict sense."

6. Domestic Networks: "Those You Count On"

1. Charles and Betty Lou Valentine have noted the existence of long-enduring networks composed of families (kindreds) and domiciles (households) in their recent study in Blackston, an Afro-American community in the Northeast (personal communication). What I have chosen to call domestic networks in this study, they call "inter-domicile, multi-family networks." Both terminologies appear to appropriately define the kin-structured domestic networks described in this study. Occasionally in this book I have synthesized the terminology and referred to "networks linking multiple domestic units."

7. Women and Men: "I'm Not in Love with No Man Really"

1. I wish to thank Professor Louise Lamphere and Professor Robert Weiss for helpful suggestions in the analysis and organization of this chapter.

8. Conclusion

1. See a report to the Subcommittee on Fiscal Policy of the Joint Economic Committee of Congress. The report, entitled "The Concept of Family in the Poor Black Community," was co-authored by Professor Herbert Semmel (Visiting Professor of Law, University of Texas School of Law) and myself.

Bibliography:

LITERATURE CITED

Abrahams, Roger. 1963. *Deep Down in the Jungle: Negro Narrative Folklore from the Streets of Philadelphia.* Hatboro, Pa.: Folklore Associates.

————. 1970a. *Deep Down in the Jungle.* Rev. ed. Chicago: Aldine Publishing Company.

————. 1970b. *Positively Black.* Englewood Cliffs, N. J.: Prentice-Hall.

Adams, L. 1960. "An Inquiry into the Nature of the Family." In *Essays on the Science of Culture,* eds. Gertrude E. Dole and R. Carneiro, New York: Thomas Y. Crowell.

Bailey, F. G. 1971. *Gifts and Poison: The Politics of Reputation.* New York: Schocken Books.

Banfield, E. C. & L. F. 1958. *Moral Basis of a Backward Society.* New York: Free Press.

Barnes, John A. 1969a. "Networks and Political Processes." In *Social Networks in Urban Situations,* ed. J. C. Mitchell. Manchester: Manchester University Press.

————. 1969b. "Graph Theory and Social Network: A Technical Comment on Connectedness and Connectivity." *Sociology,* Vol. 3: 215–232.

Barth, Frederik, ed. 1966. *The Role of the Entrepreneur in Social Change in Northern Norway.* Bergen: Norwegian University Press.

Bernard, Jessie. 1966. *Marriage and Family among Negroes.* Englewood Cliffs, N. J.: Prentice-Hall.

Billingsley, Andrew. 1968. *Black Families in White America.* Englewood Cliffs, N. J.: Prentice-Hall.

Bohannan, Paul. 1963. *Social Anthropology.* New York: Holt, Rinehart and Winston.

Boissevain, Jeremy. 1966. "Patronage in Sicily." *Man,* Journal of the Royal Anthropological Institute of Great Britain and Ireland 1 (1): 18–33.

————. 1968. "The Place of Non-Groups in the Social Sciences." *Man*, Journal of the Royal Anthropological Institute of Great Britain and Ireland 3 (4): 542–556.

Bott, Elizabeth. 1957. *Family and Social Network: Roles, Norms and External Relationships in Ordinary Urban Families*. London: Tavistock Publications.

————. 1971. *Family and Social Network*. 2d ed. New York: A Free Press Paperback.

Bryce-LaPorte, Roy S. 1971. "The Slave Plantation: Background to Present Conditions of Urban Blacks." In *Race, Change, and Urban Society*, eds. Peter Orleans and William R. Ellis. Urban Affairs Annual Reviews, No. 5. Beverly Hills, Calif.: Sage.

Buchler, Ira R., and Selby, Henry A. 1968. *Kinship and Social Organization: An Introduction to Theory and Method*. New York: Macmillan.

Bureau of the Census. 1971. Statistical Abstracts of the United States. United States Department of Commerce.

Carroll, Vern, ed. 1970. *Adoption in Eastern Oceania*. Honolulu: University of Hawaii Press.

Cicourel, Aaron V. 1964. *Method and Measurement in Sociology*. New York: The Free Press.

Dalton, George, 1961. "Economic Theory and Primitive Society. *American Anthropologist* 63:1–25.

Davenport, William H. 1959. "Nonunilineal Descent and Descent Groups." *American Anthropologist* 61:557–572.

————. 1964. "Social Structure of Santa Cruz Islands. In *Explorations in Cultural Anthropology: Essays in Honor of George Peter Murdock*, ed. W. H. Goodenough, pp. 57–93. New York: McGraw-Hill.

Denzin, Norman. 1970. *The Research Act*. Chicago: Aldine Publishing Company.

Dorson, Richard. 1956. *Negro Folktales in Michigan*. Cambridge, Mass.: Harvard University Press.

————. 1958. *Negro Tales from Pine Bluff, Arkansas, and Calvin, Michigan*. Bloomington: Indiana University Press.

Drake, St. Clair, and Cayton, Horace R. 1945. *Black Metropolis: A Study of Negro Life in a Northern City.* New York: Harcourt, Brace.

―――. 1962. *Black Metropolis.* Rev. and enlarged ed. New York: Harper & Row.

Du Bois, William E. B. 1903. *The Souls of Black Folk.* Chicago: McClurg.

Epstein, A. L. 1961. "The Network and Urban Social Organization." *Rhodes-Livingstone Journal* 29:29–62. Reprinted in *Social Networks in Urban Situations,* ed. C. Mitchell, pp. 77–116. Manchester: Manchester University Press, 1969.

Firth, Raymond; Hubert, Jane; and Forge, Anthony. 1970. *Families and Their Relatives: Kinship in a Middle-Class Sector of London.* New York: Humanities Press.

Fischer, J. L. 1958. "The Classification of Residence in Censuses." *American Anthropologist* 60:508–517.

Fortes, Meyer. 1958. Introduction. In *The Developmental Cycle in Domestic Groups,* ed. Jack Goody. Cambridge: Cambridge University Press.

―――. 1962. "Marriage in Tribal Societies." *Cambridge Papers in Social Anthropology,* No. 3. Cambridge: Cambridge University Press.

Foster, George. 1963. "The Dyadic Contract in Tzintzuntzan II: Patron-Client Relationships." *American Anthropologist* 65:1280–94.

Fox, Robin, 1967. *Kinship and Marriage.* Baltimore: Penguin Books.

Frazier, E. Franklin. 1939. *The Negro Family in the United States.* Chicago: University of Chicago Press.

Gonzalez, Nancie. 1965. "The Consanguineal Household and Matrifocality." *American Anthropologist* 67:1541–1549.

―――. 1969. *Black Carib Household Structure: A Study of Migration and Modernization.* Seattle: University of Washington Press.

―――. 1970. "Toward a Definition of Matrifocality." In *Afro-American Anthropology: Contemporary Perspectives,* eds. N. E. Whitten and John F. Szwed. New York: The Free Press.

Goodenough, Ward H. 1962. "Kindred and Hamlet in Lakalai, New Britain." *Ethnology* 1:5–12.

———. 1965. "Rethinking Status and Role." In *The Relevance of Models for Social Anthropology*, ed. M. Banton. London: Tavistock Press.

———. 1970. *Description and Comparison in Cultural Anthropology*. Chicago: Aldine Publishing Company.

Goody, Esther. 1966. "Fostering of Children in Ghana: A Preliminary Report." *Ghana Journal of Sociology* 2:26–33.

Gough, Kathleen. 1959. "The Nayars and the Definition of Marriage." *Journal of the Royal Anthropological Institute* 89:23–24.

———. 1961. "Nayar: Central Kerala." In *Matrilineal Kinship*, eds. D. M. Schneider and K. Gough, pp. 298–384. Berkeley and Los Angeles: University of California Press.

Gouldner, Alvin W. 1960. "The Norm of Reciprocity: A Preliminary Statement." *American Sociological Review* 25:161–178.

Hannerz, Ulf. 1969. *Soulside: Inquiries into Ghetto Culture and Community*. New York: Columbia University Press.

Harrington, Michael. 1962. *The Other America*. New York: Macmillan.

Harris, Marvin. 1971. *Culture, Man, and Nature: An Introduction to General Anthropology*. New York: Thomas Y. Crowell.

Helm, June. 1965. "Bilaterality in the Socio-Territorial Organization of the Arctic Drain Age Dene." *Ethnology*, Vol. 4, pp. 361–385.

Johnson, Charles S. 1941. *Growing Up in the Black Belt*. American Council on Education.

Keesing, Roger M. 1966. "Kwaio Kindreds." *Southwestern Journal of Anthropology* 22:346–355.

———. 1969. "On Quibblings over Squabblings of Siblings: New Perspectives on Kin Terms and Role Behavior." *Southwestern Journal of Anthropology* 25:207–227.

———. 1970a. "Kwaio Fosterage." *American Anthropologist* 72(5):991–1020.

———. 1970b. "Toward a Model of Role Analysis." In *A Handbook of Methods in Cultural Anthropology*, eds. R. Cohen and R. Naroll. New York: Natural History Press.

Keil, Charles. 1966. *Urban Blues.* Chicago: University of Chicago Press.

Kunstadter, P. 1963. "A Survey of the Consanguine or Matrifocal Family." *American Anthropologist* 65:56–66.

Ladner, Joyce A. 1971. *Tomorrow's Tomorrow: The Black Woman.* Garden City: N. Y.: Doubleday.

Lee, Richard B. 1969. "Kung Bushman Subsistence: An Input-Output Analysis." In *Environment and Culture Behavior: Ecological Studies in Cultural Anthropology*, ed. A. P. Vayda, pp. 47–79. New York: Natural History Press.

Lévi-Strauss, Claude. 1969. *The Elementary Structures of Kinship.* Boston: Beacon Press (first published 1949).

Lewis, Hylan. 1967. "The Family: Resources for Change," Agenda Paper, Planning Session, White House Conference, "To Fulfill These Rights," 1965. Reprinted in *The Moynihan Report: The Politics of Controversy*, eds. L. Rainwater and W. Yancy. Cambridge, M.I.T. Press.

————. 1967. "Culture, Class and Family Life among Low Income Urban Negroes," in *Employment, Race, Poverty*, eds. M. Ross and H. Hill. New York. Harcourt, Brace & World.

————. 1971. "The Culture of Poverty: What does It Matter?" in *The Culture of Poverty: A Critique*, ed. E. Leacock. New York. Simon and Schuster.

Lewis, Oscar. 1950. "An Anthropological Approach to Family Studies." *American Journal of Sociology*, Vol. LV, No. 5, pp. 467–475.

————. 1959. *Five Families: Mexican Case Studies in the Culture of Poverty.* New York: Basic Books.

————. 1966a. *La Vida: A Puerto Rican Family in the Culture of Poverty—San Juan and New York.* New York: Random House.

————. 1966b. "The Culture of Poverty." *Scientific American* 215 (4):19–25.

Liebow, Elliot. 1967. *Tally's Corner: A Study of Negro Streetcorner Men.* Boston: Little, Brown.

Lombardi, John R. 1973. "Exchange and Survival." Preprint. Boston: Boston University.

Malinowski, Bronislaw. 1922. *Argonauts of the Western Pacific*. New York: Dutton.

————. 1930. "Parenthood—The Basis of Social Structure." In *The New Generation*, eds. V. F. Calverston and Samuel D. Schmalhausen. pp. 113–168. New York: Macauley.

Mauss, Marcel. 1925. "Essai sur le don: Forme et raison de l'échange dans les sociétés archaïques." *Année Sociologique*, n.s., I:30–186.

————. 1954. *The Gift*. New York: The Free Press.

Midgett, Douglas K. 1969. "Transactions in Parenthood: A West Indian Case." Unpublished ms., University of Illinois.

Mitchell, J. Clyde. 1966. "Theoretical Orientations in African Urban Studies." In *The Social Anthropology of Complex Societies*, ed. Michael Banton. A.S.A. Monograph, No. 4, pp. 37–68. London: Tavistock Publications.

Mitchell, William E. 1963. "Theoretical Problems in the Concept of the Kindred." *American Anthropologist* 65: 343–354.

Moynihan, Daniel Patrick. 1965. "The Negro Family: The Case for National Action." Washington, D.C.: U.S. Government Printing Office. Prepared for the Office of Policy Planning and Research of the Department of Labor.

Murdock, George. 1949. *Social Structure*. New York: Macmillan.

Myrdal, Gunnar. 1944. *An American Dilemma: The Negro Problem and Modern Democracy*. New York: Harper & Row.

Otterbein, Keith F. 1970. "The Developmental Cycle of the Andros Household: A Diachronic Analysis." *American Anthropologist* 72(6):1412–1419.

Piven, Frances Fox and Richard A. Cloward. 1971. *Regulating the Poor: The Functions of Public Welfare*. New York: Vintage Books.

Radcliffe-Brown, A. R. 1950. Introduction. In *African Systems of Kinship and Marriage*, eds. A. R. Radcliffe-Brown and C. D. Forde. London: Oxford University Press.

Rainwater, Lee. 1966. "Crucible of Identity: The Negro Lower-Class Family." *Daedalus* 95(2):172–216.

Richards, A. I. 1950. "Some Types of Family Structure amongst the Central Bantu." In *African Systems of Kinship and Marriage*, eds. A. R. Radcliffe-Brown and C. D. Forde, London: Oxford University Press, pp. 207–251.

Rivers, W. H. 1924. *Social Organization*. New York: Knopf.

Rodman, Hyman. 1971. *Lower-Class Families: The Culture of Poverty in Negro Trinidad*. London: Oxford University Press.

Ryan, William. 1971. *Blaming the Victim*. New York: Random House.

Sahlins, Marshall D. 1965. "On the Sociology of Primitive Exchange." In *The Relevance of Models for Social Anthropology*, ed. Michael Banton. A.S.A. Monograph I. London: Tavistock Publications; New York: Praeger.

Sanford, Margaret Sellars. 1971. "Disruption of the Mother-Child Relationship in Conjunction with Matrifocality: A Study of Child-Keeping among the Carib and Creole of British Honduras." Ph.D. dissertation, The Catholic University of America. Anthropology Studies 19, Ms.

Scheffler, Harold W. 1970. "Kinship and Adoption in the Northern New Hebrides." In *Adoption in Eastern Oceania*, ed. V. Carroll, pp. 369–383. Honolulu: University of Hawaii Press.

Schneider, David M. 1968. *American Kinship: A Cultural Account*. Englewood Cliffs, N. J.: Prentice-Hall.

Schneider, David, and Gough, K. 1961. *Matrilineal Kinship*. Berkeley and Los Angeles: University of California Press.

Schulz, David. 1969. *Coming Up Black: Patterns of Ghetto Socialization*. Englewood Cliffs, N.J.: Prentice-Hall.

Smith, Raymond T. 1970. "The Nuclear Family in Afro-American Kinship." *Journal of Comparative Family Studies* 1(1):55–70.

Stack, Carol B. 1970. "The Kindred of Viola Jackson: Residence and Family Organization of an Urban Black American Family." In *Afro-American Anthropology: Contemporary Perspectives*, eds. N. E. Whitten and John F. Szwed. New York: The Free Press, pp. 303–312.

State of Illinois. 1965. "Public Aid in Illinois." Published by Department of Public Aid.

———. 1970. "Public Aid in Illinois." Published by Department of Public Aid.

Steiner, Gilbert Y. 1971. *The State of Welfare.* Washington, D.C.: The Brookings Institution.

Strauss, Anselm L. 1959. *Mirrors and Masks: The Search for Identity.* New York: The Free Press.

Valentine, Charles A. 1968. *Culture and Poverty: Critique and Counterproposals.* Chicago: University of Chicago Press.

———. 1970. "Blackston: Progress Report on a Community Study in Urban Afro-America." Mimeographed. St. Louis: Washington University.

———. 1971. "Deficit, Difference, and Bicultural Models of Afro-American Behavior." *Harvard Educational Review,* Vol. 41, No. 2, May.

———. 1972. "Black Studies and Anthropology: Scholarly and Political Interests in Afro-American Culture." An Addison-Wesley Module in Anthropology, No. 15, Reading, Mass.: Addison-Wesley.

Whitten, N. E., and Szwed, John F., eds. 1970. *Afro-American Anthropology: Contemporary Perspectives.* New York: The Free Press.

Whitten, N. E., and Wolfe, Alvin W. 1972. "Network Analysis." In *The Handbook of Social and Cultural Anthropology,* ed. John J. Honigmann. Chicago: Rand-McNally, in press.

Willhelm, Sidney M. 1971. *Who Needs the Negro?* Garden City, N. Y. Doubleday (Anchor).

Young, M. and Willmott, P. 1957. *Family and Kinship in East London.* London: Routledge and Kegan Paul.

Index